C000142233

Grappling with God

with God

**Explorations of the Old Testament
for personal and small group use**

BOOK ONE

Law and promise

Nick Fawcett

Kevin
Mayhew

First published in 2000 by
KEVIN MAYHEW LTD
Buxhall
Stowmarket
Suffolk IP14 3BW

© 2000 Nick Fawcett

The right of Nick Fawcett to be identified as the author
of this work has been asserted by him in accordance
with the Copyright, Designs and Patents Act 1988.

All rights reserved. No part of this publication may be
reproduced, stored in a retrieval system, or transmitted,
in any form or by any means, electronic, mechanical,
photocopying, recording or otherwise, without the
prior written permission of the publisher.

0 1 2 3 4 5 6 7 8 9

ISBN 1 84003 499 8
Catalogue No 1500331

Cover design by Jonathan Stroulger
Edited by Katherine Laidler
Typesetting by Louise Selfe

Printed and bound in Great Britain

To my parents-in-law, Michael and Marina Sanders,
with thanks for their unfailing support and encouragement

About the author

Nick Fawcett was born in 1957. He studied Theology at Bristol University and Regent's Park College, Oxford. His early years of ministry were spent in Somerset and Lancashire, and from 1989 to 1996 he was Minister of Gas Green Baptist Church, Cheltenham. From November 1996 to June 1999 he served as Toc H Chaplain and Development Officer for Wales and the West of England.

He is now concentrating full-time on his career as a writer, proof-reader and indexer. His books to date are *No Ordinary Man* (1997), *Prayers For All Seasons* (1998), *Are You Listening?* (1998) and *Getting It Across* (1999), all published by Kevin Mayhew. He has also written the texts for the *Best Loved Choral Melodies Choral Collection* (1999) and had four hymns chosen for inclusion in the Churches Together Millennium Hymn Book *New Start Hymns and Songs* (1999), both also published by Kevin Mayhew.

He lives with his wife, Deborah, and their two young children, Samuel and Katie, in Wellington, Somerset.

Acknowledgements

I am indebted in the writing of this book to my wife, Deborah, for her invaluable help and support; to Katherine Laidler for all the time and work she has put in to editing the manuscript; to Peter Dainty for his invariably constructive comments and criticisms; and to Kevin Mayhew Publishers for the opportunity to put this and other material into print.

Scripture quotations are taken from the New Revised Standard Version of the Bible, copyright 1989 by the Division of Christian Education of the National Council of the Churches of Christ in the USA. Used by permission. All rights reserved.

Proverbs are taken from *The Penguin Book of Proverbs* and *Collins Gem Dictionary of Quotations*. Unless otherwise stated, the source is unknown.

The extract from the speech by Martin Luther King is reproduced by kind permission of Laurence Pollinger Limited and the Estate of Martin Luther King.

Contents

Introduction _____

Why read the Old Testament? If I had a pound for every time I've been asked that question I would be a rich man indeed. Many people feel that it is superfluous to their requirements; a confusing and sometimes disturbing book which they feel is best left unexplored. And though I believe they are mistaken, I can understand how they reach that conclusion, for there is much in the Old Testament which is difficult to come to terms with – a multitude of passages which can seem either dull, primitive or downright barbaric by Christian standards. It is often hard to reconcile the God we find there with the God we believe has been revealed to us in Jesus Christ.

Yet to abandon the Old Testament because of such difficulties is to deny oneself untold riches. Imagine Christmas or Holy Week without the great words of the prophet Isaiah: 'The people who walked in darkness have seen a great light'; 'He was wounded for our transgressions, crushed for our iniquities; upon him was the punishment that made us whole.' Imagine Good Friday without the unforgettable cry of the Psalmist: 'My God, my God, why have you forsaken me?' Imagine Pentecost without the wonderful vision of Joel: 'Your sons and daughters shall prophesy, your old men shall dream dreams, and your young men shall see visions.' Like it or not, the Christian faith has its roots firmly in the Old Testament, and it is in the light of its pages that, at least in part, the testimony of the New must be interpreted.

The Old Testament, however, has more to offer than simply words of prophecy. It records some of the most unforgettable stories ever told: Noah and the Great Flood, Esau and Jacob, Moses crossing the Red Sea, Samson and Delilah, David and Goliath, Daniel in the lions' den, Shadrach, Meshach and Abednego, Jonah and the 'whale' – and so we could go on. Here are tales which have captured the imagination of people across the centuries, and rightly so, for as well as communicating deep theological truths they also speak directly to our human condition. Time and again we can identify with the characters in question, seeing something of ourselves in each one. It is, perhaps, in the raw human emotions so often displayed and the almost brutal honesty before God that the Old Testament's greatest strength lies. So much of what we see there mirrors what we feel and experience ourselves.

Every individual will approach the complexities thrown up by the Old Testament in their own way. For me they reflect a nation's grappling with God across the centuries. From a crude awareness of God way back in the mists of time, we move inexorably forward to an ever-deepening understanding of his greatness, love and mercy, all brought together in the anticipation of the promised Messiah. Not that the coming of Jesus means our picture of God is complete, for we too must wrestle in our turn if we are to move forward in our journey of faith. God may be fully revealed in Christ, but for now we see only in part. Like his people of old, we must press on towards the kingdom he holds in store.

This book is one of a series of four which together take us briefly through the pages of the Old Testament. In this volume we look at the first five books of the Bible and dip also into the book of Joshua, moving from Creation to the founding fathers of the Jewish nation, from the Great Flood to the giving of the Law, from the promise given to Abraham to the first tentative steps into the Promised Land. As with each of the other volumes, the meditations you will find here give just a taste of the great wealth of stories to be found in these early pages of Scripture. Many of those which are covered are associated with complex theological issues which are beyond the scope of a book such as this. The aim, rather, is to draw the reader into the stories so that they feel part of the incidents related. Necessarily many questions will be left unanswered, but if anything in the pages which follow brings home the challenge of the Old Testament for today, then I believe I will have been true to the overriding intention of all Scripture.

Each of the volumes in this collection is designed both for individual and group use. You may find them helpful in your personal devotions, or equally they may provide material for a Bible study or house group. The themed 'chapters' have been set out with both ends in mind. They begin with an introductory paragraph which sets the scene for what follows. A scriptural reading then leads into a meditation, exploring the incidents related from the perspective of the principal character involved. The remaining sections are all designed to aid further reflection. First, a selection of proverbs related to what has gone before is offered as food for thought. The relevance of some of these will be obvious, of others less so, but make time to consider their truth or otherwise. What does each one have to say about the subject? Do they aid understanding or confuse the issue? Do they sum up the key theme or point in an altogether different direction? This leads on to questions for discussion or personal reflection. There is no right or wrong answer to many of these questions; rather they are designed to help apply what the Bible has to say to our own lives. Don't rush through them with a cursory 'yes' or 'no'; ask yourself what each one is driving at and whether perhaps some have a challenge for you. Finally, additional passages of Scripture are recommended which may help you consider further the issues which have been raised; issues which are summed up in a concluding prayer.

The Old Testament is not an easy book to read, but it more than repays those who work at understanding what it has to say. It is my hope that through this collection of readings, prayers and meditations, familiar and not so familiar stories will come alive in new and unexpected ways.

Nick Fawcett

Opening prayer _____

Living God,
    there comes a time for us all
    when we must meet your challenge and respond –
    a time when, try as we might,
    we can no longer go on running from your presence.
The experience can be painful and disturbing –
    facing ourselves as we really are,
    looking into the darker recesses of our minds,
    and measuring all this against your infinite goodness.
We prefer to stifle the voice of conscience,
    to avoid the uncomfortable
    and deny what we would rather not accept,
    but until we make our peace with you
    we can find no rest for our souls.
Give us, then, the courage
    to wrestle with you in the wilderness
    until our doubts are resolved,
    our reservations overcome
    and our sins dealt with.
So may we experience for ourselves
    the blessings which you alone can give.
In the name of Christ. Amen.

There is nothing patent in the New Testament
that is not latent in the Old.
(Anon)

1 Excuses, excuses! _____

_____ *Adam*

There can be few passages of Scripture which have created such heated debate as the opening chapters of Genesis. While some, even today, argue for a strictly literal interpretation of the text, others maintain it refers to humankind in general, its aim being to communicate fundamental theological truths. No doubt debate will continue, but, however you approach them, the Creation narratives in Genesis, and the account of 'The Fall' in particular, point graphically to certain key aspects of human nature. In one sense, at least, Adam and Eve represent us all: in their instinctive attempts to shift blame for their actions on to someone or something other than themselves. And the irony is that, more often than not, we, like Adam, are unaware of doing so.

Reading – Genesis 3:1-13

Now the serpent was more crafty than any other wild animal that the Lord God had made. He said to the woman, 'Did God say, "You shall not eat from any tree in the garden"?' The woman said to the serpent, 'We may eat of the fruit of the trees in the garden; but God said, "You shall not eat of the fruit of the tree that is in the middle of the garden, nor shall you touch it, or you shall die".' But the serpent said to the woman, 'You will not die; for God knows that when you eat of it your eyes will be opened, and you will be like God knowing good and evil.' So when the woman saw that the tree was good for food, and that it was a delight to the eyes, and that the tree was to be desired to make one wise, she took of its fruit and ate; and she also gave some to her husband, who was with her, and he ate. Then the eyes of both were opened, and they knew that they were naked; and they sewed fig leaves together and made loincloths for themselves.

They heard the sound of the Lord God walking in the garden at the time of the evening breeze, and the man and his wife hid themselves from the presence of the Lord God among the trees of the garden. But the Lord God called to the man, and said to him, 'Where are you?' He said, 'I heard the sound of you in the garden, and I was afraid, because I was naked; and I hid myself.' He said, 'Who told you that you were naked? Have you eaten from the tree of which I commanded you not to eat?' The man said, 'The woman whom you gave to be with me, she gave me fruit from the tree, and I ate.' Then the Lord God said to the woman, 'What is this that you have done?' The woman said, 'The serpent tricked me, and I ate.'

Meditation

Don't blame me, it wasn't my fault!
All right, I did wrong –
    I can see that now, looking back –
    but at the time there seemed no harm in it,
    certainly nothing to get steamed up about.
Just one tiny fruit, that's all it was,
    so why the fuss?
It wasn't my idea either, that's what makes it worse –
    it was that wretched woman,
    the one God supposedly gave me for company.
Some help she turned out to be!
'Go on,' she said, 'just one bite. It won't hurt.'
I tried to refuse, honestly,
    but she wouldn't take no for an answer,
    teasing,
    tempting,
    sulking,
    pleading,
    until at last, against my better judgement, I gave in,
    anything for a bit of peace.
Yes, I should have been stronger,
    I can't quibble with that.
I should have listened to the voice of conscience
    and done what I knew to be right.
But I didn't, and it's too late now for regrets,
    hard done by though I've been.
I was pushed into it,
    a victim of circumstance,
    caught up in a web outside my own making.
Not that it was all down to Eve –
    no, it's God I ultimately blame.
What was he thinking of,
    putting that tree there in the first place?
There was no need, surely?
We had enough and more than enough,

so why put temptation in our way?
He must have known the risks –
    probably even saw our fall coming –
    so what chance did we have,
    what hope of sticking to the straight and narrow?
No, if you ask me, we got a raw deal,
    almost, you might say, a miscarriage of justice.
But give me credit,
    however wronged I may have been,
    however unfairly treated,
    there's one thing I can promise you:
    you won't catch me making excuses –
    not likely!

To ponder

- Every man is the architect of his own fortune.
- He who excuses himself, accuses himself.
- Bad excuses are worse than none.
- The absent party is always to blame.
- Everyone puts his fault on the times.
- When one falls, it is not one's foot that is to blame. *(Chinese proverb)*
- When the fruit is scarcest, its taste is sweetest. *(Irish proverb)*

To discuss

- Confessing our faults to God is easy . . . or is it? Do we genuinely admit our mistakes to him, or deep down have we already made excuses for our actions, expecting him to do the same?
- We may think we recognise our own faults and weaknesses, but do we? Is it possible to make excuses without even realising we are doing it, particularly when there are truths about ourselves which we would rather not face?
- Confessing our faults to God and even ourselves is one thing; admitting them to someone else, especially someone close to us, quite another. Why is this so often true? What do we find so hard in acknowledging our faults before others?

To consider further

Read James 1:12-18, and ask yourself what, in the light of the story of Adam, these verses are saying to you.

Prayer

Lord,
   we don't like being wrong.
It hurts our pride and goes against the grain
   to admit we've made a mistake.
Far easier to blame somebody else,
   to look for a reason which excuses our actions.
'We were forced into it', we tell ourselves,
   'our hands tied . . . ',
   but deep down we know
   that the responsibility to choose is ours,
   no one else's,
   each of us answerable for our own actions.
Forgive us, Lord,
   for those times we have shifted the blame
   on to others.
Forgive us
   for hiding behind falsehoods and half-truths
   rather than being honest with ourselves.
And forgive us
   for letting such excuses become so much part of us
   we no longer realise we are making them.
Teach us to make our own decisions
   wisely and with integrity;
   and when we go wrong,
   give us courage to admit it,
   and humility to accept our dependence
   on your unfailing grace.
Amen.

2 Fallen creation _____

_____ *God*

When the idea was first put to me of including a 'meditation of God' exploring the theme of creation, I was hesitant to say the least. Who am I to claim insight into the workings of the divine mind? The answer, of course, is that I have no more knowledge than anyone else. What follows, then, in no way claims special insight into the spiritual complexities of our universe. On the contrary, it speaks rather of the fact that God's ways are not our ways, nor his thoughts our thoughts. The more I tried to make sense of his design and purpose in creation, the more I became aware of my inability to do so. With God, as with life itself, we are repeatedly confronted by unfathomable mysteries, and only a fool imagines they can solve more than the merest few. Yet grappling with the issues such questions raise, whilst profoundly unsettling, is also immensely rewarding for it reminds us that God is not remote and detached from his creation, but intimately involved with its future.

Reading – Genesis 3:14-19, 22-24

The Lord God said to the serpent, 'Because you have done this, cursed are you among all animals and among all wild creatures; upon your belly you shall go, and dust you shall eat all the days of your life. I will put enmity between you and the woman, and between your offspring and hers; he will strike your head, and you will strike his heel.'

To the woman he said, 'I will greatly increase your pangs in child-bearing; in pain you shall bring forth children, yet your desire shall be for your husband, and he shall rule over you.'

And to the man he said, 'Because you have listened to the voice of your wife, and have eaten of the tree about which I commanded you, "You shall not eat of it," cursed is the ground because of you; in toil you shall eat of it all the days of your life; thorns and thistles it shall bring forth for you; and you shall eat the plants of the field. By the sweat of your face you shall eat bread until you return to the ground, for out of it you were taken; you are dust, and to dust you shall return.'

Then the Lord God said, 'See, the man has become like one of us, knowing good and evil; and now, he might reach out his hand and take also from the tree of life, and eat, and live for ever' – therefore the

Lord God sent him forth from the garden of Eden, to till the ground from which he was taken. He drove out the man; and at the east of the garden of Eden he placed the cherubim, and a sword flaming and turning to guard the way to the tree of life.

Meditation

What have I done?
What *have* I done?
Day after day I look at the world I've made,
   intended to be so beautiful,
   so special,
   and I see hatred,
   violence,
   greed,
   corruption –
   so much that maims and mutilates,
   destroying hope,
   denying life.
Can you imagine what it feels like,
   living with the awfulness of ultimate responsibility,
   and bearing that burden not just for a fleeting span
   but for all eternity?
I don't think you can.
But, believe me, whatever pain you've endured,
   whatever sorrow,
   whatever heartbreak,
   it can never touch the agony
   of watching your creation slowly tearing itself apart.
Was it all a mistake?
Some will say so, and I can't blame them.
Yet I had love to give and life to share –
   would it have been any more moral to keep that to myself.
I could, of course, have made you like puppets,
   every thought controlled,
   every action directed,
   but is that what you'd have wanted? –
   unable to think or feel,
   deprived of joy for lack of sorrow,
   of love for lack of hate,
   of hope for lack of fear,
   of pleasure for lack of pain.

Don't tell me I'm not to blame,
    for it just won't do.
I made you, didn't I? –
    mine the hand that brought you into being,
    so though the mistakes may be yours
    the fault surely is mine?
Yet don't think I've given up on you,
    for, perfect or imperfect,
    I love you just the same,
    and I'm going to go on loving for as long as it takes,
    giving my all for you,
    my very life,
    until the broken threads of creation
    are woven together into a glorious new tapestry,
    and we are one, you and I,
    united in paradise,
    now and for ever.

To ponder

- God moves in a mysterious way.
- God gives, but he does not lock the gate of the fold. *(Bulgarian proverb)*
- If the beginning is good, the end must be perfect.
- That never ends ill which begins in God's name.

To discuss

- Would there be any point to life without free will?
- Each day children are born into the world, even though their parents know life will bring them sorrow as well as joy. Does this give us any insight into God's gift of life to us?

To consider further

Read Romans 8:18-25 and Revelation 21:1-4. What do these passages say to you about creation and God's purpose within it?

Prayer

God of all,
    we look at our world sometimes –
    at its suffering and sorrow,
    its hurt and heartbreak –
    and we don't understand why you let it happen.
We see hatred and evil,
    greed and corruption,
    so much that frustrates your will
    and denies your purpose,
    and we cannot help but ask,
    where are you in the face of it?
Our minds struggle
    to take in the great mysteries of life
    for we ourselves are a part of your fallen creation.
Yet though we cannot always make sense of your will,
    we believe that your nature is love
    and that the time will come
    when our questions will be answered
    and your purpose revealed.
Until then, help us to live with paradox
    and trust in your eternal promises,
    knowing that every moment of every day
    you are at work,
    striving to bring creation to perfection.
Amen.

3 Fruits of anger

Cain

There's an old saying, 'When anger arises, think of the consequences' – a variation of 'Stop, and count to ten'. But while the advice may be familiar, and the sense behind it plain to see, when the moment comes we all too easily forget it. The trouble with anger is that it clouds our vision, making even the most mild-mannered of people act entirely out of character. The consequences can be disastrous for all concerned. In the story of Cain and Abel we find not only anger let loose, but envy also – another basic yet enormously destructive human emotion. The resultant cocktail proves lethal!

Reading – Genesis 4:2b-10

Now Abel was a keeper of sheep, and Cain a tiller of the ground. In the course of time Cain brought to the Lord an offering of the fruit of the ground, and Abel for his part brought of the firstlings of his flock, their fat portions. And the Lord had regard for Abel and his offering, but for Cain and his offering he had no regard. So Cain was very angry, and his countenance fell. The Lord said to Cain, 'Why are you angry, and why has your countenance fallen? If you do well, will you not be accepted? And if you do not do well, sin is lurking at the door; its desire is for you, but you must master it.'

Cain said to his brother Abel, 'Let us go out to the field.' And when they were in the field, Cain rose up against his brother Abel, and killed him. Then the Lord said to Cain, 'Where is your brother Abel?' He said, 'I do not know; am I my brother's keeper?' And the Lord said, 'What have you done? Listen; your brother's blood is crying out to me from the ground!'

Meditation

If only I'd listened,
    allowed time for my temper to cool,
    how different it might have been.
He tried to warn me,

but I wouldn't listen,
    too piqued at my gift being snubbed,
    too full of resentment to listen to reason.
It seemed so unfair, that was the trouble,
    for I'd made my offering in good faith –
    the best of my crop,
    specially selected,
    fit for a prince –
    so when God turned it down I was furious,
    more hurt than I can tell you.
What was wrong with it, I wanted to know?
Why was Abel's gift accepted
    and mine turned down?
It was one law for him and another for me,
    that's how it seemed.
And somehow, the more I thought about it,
    the more it got to me,
    nagging away like a festering wound.
Was he gloating, I wondered,
    sniggering slyly behind my back?
Or worse, was he feeling sorry for me,
    striving to keep the look of pity from his eyes?
It was quite unfounded, of course,
    all a phantom of my fevered imagination,
    but once the seed was sown
    there was no controlling it,
    suspicion growing out of all proportion
    until I could think of nothing else.
And as the sense of injustice mounted within me,
    so too did the anger,
    a dark and ugly cloud, full of menace.
I wanted revenge,
    to vent my spleen,
    so I lured him out into the fields,
    determined to confront him.
Did I mean to kill him?
I like to think not.
I was going to knock him about a bit,
    that's what I tell myself,
    teach him a lesson,
    show him who was boss,
    but when rage was let loose it ran amok –
    blind to reason,

blind to everything.
He had no idea what was coming,
   that's what haunts me.
As we walked out together,
   my hand on his shoulder,
   there was no hint of mistrust,
   not even the slightest hesitation;
   just a look of innocent enquiry –
   but it served only to fan the flames,
   and with one blow I struck him down.
I thought the sentence harsh afterwards,
   even presumed to complain, would you believe?
As though I deserved better,
   sympathy,
   understanding.
Little did I realise the punishment yet to come,
   for I've had to live since then,
   day after day,
   with the knowledge of my foul crime,
   and that memory will stay with me,
   torturing my soul,
   until the day I die.
Lord, have mercy upon me.

To ponder

- Anger punishes itself.
- Anger begins with folly, and ends with repentance.
- Anger is a short madness.
- Anger restrained is wisdom gained.
- Two things a man should never be angry at; what he can help, and what he cannot help.
- When anger arises, think of the consequences.

To discuss

- Reading between the lines, can you think of any reasons why Cain's offering was not accepted by God?
- Anger and jealousy may not lead to murder, but they can have many other negative consequences. What are they?
- What ways of controlling anger have you found most helpful?

To consider further

Read Matthew 5:21-26, Ephesians 4:26-7 and James 1:19-20. Compare the message of these verses with the story of Cain and Abel; then ask yourself what God is saying to you.

Prayer

Gracious God,
    you are slow to anger,
    swift to bless,
    full of mercy,
    abounding in love.
Forgive us that we are so different,
    easily roused,
    reluctant to let go of a grievance,
    unwilling to forgive,
    grudging in showing affection.
Forgive us all those times
    we have nursed bitterness in our hearts,
    resentful of the success or good fortune of others.
Forgive us those many occasions
    we have acted foolishly,
    living to regret mistakes made in haste.
Help us to recognise
    that envy has no place in our lives,
    serving only to poison and destroy.
And help us to recognise equally
    that, though anger may sometimes be justified,
    we must learn also to control it
    before *it* controls *us*.
Amen.

4 The foolishness of faith

Noah

There are few of us who like to stand out from the crowd, least of all when it involves being radically different. The occasional foible is one thing, eccentricity quite another. No one likes to be thought odd. Yet when Noah set to work building an ark in the middle of the wilderness he must have looked exactly that – a strange character if ever there was one. It's hard to imagine the ridicule he must have been subjected to day after day as he laboured on his extraordinary enterprise with no sign of rain let alone flood. Given all that, it is tempting to suggest Noah had the last laugh, but I suspect laughter was the last thing on his mind after the tragedy which followed. The story of Noah is not about saying 'I told you so' to a cynical and hostile world. It is rather about having the courage to be different in the hope that someone, somewhere, may perhaps take notice.

Reading – Genesis 6:11-22

Now the earth was corrupt in God's sight and the earth was filled with violence. And God saw that the earth was corrupt; for all flesh had corrupted its ways upon the earth. And God said to Noah, 'I have determined to make an end of all flesh, for the earth is filled with violence because of them; now I am going to destroy them along with the earth. Make yourself an ark of cypress wood; make rooms in the ark, and cover it inside and out with pitch. This is how you are to make it: the length of the ark three hundred cubits, its width fifty cubits, and its height thirty cubits. Make a roof for the ark, and finish it to a cubit above; and put the door of the ark in its side; make it with lower, second, and third decks. For my part, I am going to bring a flood of waters on the earth, to destroy from under heaven all flesh in which is the breath of life; everything that is on the earth shall die. But I will establish my covenant with you; and you shall come into the ark, you, your sons, your wife, and your sons' wives with you. And of every living thing, of all flesh, you shall bring two of every kind into the ark, to keep them alive with you; they shall be male and female. Of the birds according to their kinds, and of the animals according to their kinds, of every creeping thing of the ground according to its kind, two of every kind shall come in to you, to keep them alive. Also take with you every kind of food that is eaten, and store it up; and it shall serve as food for you and for them.' Noah did this; he did all that God commanded him.

Meditation

'A right one we've got here!'
That's what they were thinking,
   and, quite frankly, I could hardly blame them.
Let's face it, building a boat in the middle of the desert,
    it's not something you see every day, is it? –
    an unusual hobby to put it mildly.
So it wasn't long before a crowd gathered
   and the laughter started,
     playful at first,
     good-natured banter mostly,
    but before long turning ugly.
They realised I was serious, I suppose,
   that I actually expected to use the thing,
   and that's when everything changed –
    first the sarcasm,
    then the insults,
    then the downright abuse.
'Who do you think you are?' they shouted.
'Get off your high horse you smug-faced hypocrite!'
I can repeat that bit – not the rest –
   but when I tell you
   we had to keep watch through the night,
   maybe that gives some idea of what I faced.
It was hard, believe me,
   and there were times, many times,
   when I felt like giving up,
   abandoning the whole thing
   and taking my chance with the rest.
What if I was wrong, I asked myself.
What if I'd dreamt the whole thing up?
A right fool I'd look then.
It may sound heroic looking back,
   but, believe me, there's nothing pleasant
   about being the odd one out –
   when you're the one on the spot

I can assure you it's no joke.
Yet I believed God had spoken,
    that he'd called me to respond in faith,
    and when I looked around me –
    at the state of society,
    evil and injustice everywhere –
    there was only one option,
    only one response I could possibly make.
Not that I took any pleasure in what happened next –
    when the wind blew and the storms began,
    when the rain fell and the floods rose –
    men, women, children everywhere –
    yelling,
    screaming,
    sobbing,
    dying.
It was awful,
    a sight I pray never to see again,
    and despite what some may say,
    I swear it broke God's heart as much as mine.
It could have been me, that's the sobering thing –
    had I given in to the pressure,
    swallowed my principles and followed the crowd,
    I'd have shared the same fate –
    me and my loved ones.
They thought I was mad,
    a religious nutcase,
    and I'd begun to believe they might be right;
    but I realise now,
    painful though the lesson was,
    that to this world, all too often,
    the wisdom of God looks like foolishness.

To ponder

- God provides for him who trusts.
- Our own actions are our security, not others' judgements.
- The shortest answer is doing.
- The wise forget insults, as the ungrateful a kindness.
- Many can bear adversity, but few contempt.

To discuss

- Should Christians stand out from people around them, or should they attempt to appear as 'normal' as possible? Why?
- Why do people ridicule and even persecute those who seem different?
- Are there times when faith seems foolish? What are they, and what makes you feel as you do in such situations?

To consider further

Read 1 Corinthians 1:20-31. In what do you put your trust: human wisdom or God's foolishness?

Prayer

Loving God,
    you call us to distinctive discipleship,
    a way of life that sets us apart from others;
    not a self-righteous superiority
    based on judgemental intolerance,
    but a quality of love and willingness to serve
    which shows itself in everything we say and do.
Forgive us that we fall so far short of that calling,
    compromising what we believe for fear of mockery.
Forgive us that we go along with the way of the crowd
    rather than follow the demanding way of Christ.
Speak to us now,
    challenge our complacency,
    and give us the courage to be different.
Amen.

5 Facing the unknown _____

_____ *Abram*

What are you most scared of? Spiders? Snakes? The dark? Possibly even all of these? But, according to those who claim to know, there is one thing probably all of us are scared of still more, and that, quite simply, is the unknown. Familiarity may breed contempt, but it also brings a sense of security, the thought of venturing out into uncharted waters a daunting challenge which most of us prefer to avoid. It can be traumatic enough moving to a new house or starting a new job – any change more radical than that can be bewildering indeed. Yet this was the challenge faced by Abram, later to be called Abraham. Comfortably settled in the town of Haran, he suddenly felt a call to move on. The destination was unclear, as were any details of what he might find when he got there. This was to be a step into the unknown, a journey of faith. No wonder Abraham has been held up as a paradigm of faith ever since.

Reading – Genesis 12:1-5a

Now the Lord said to Abram, 'Go from your country and your kindred and your father's house to the land that I will show you. I will make of you a great nation, and I will bless you, and make your name great, so that you will be a blessing. I will bless those who bless you, and the one who curses you I will curse; and in you all the families of the earth shall be blessed.'

So Abram went, as the Lord had told him; and Lot went with him. Abram was seventy-five years old when he departed from Haran. Abram took his wife Sarai and his brother's son Lot, and all the possessions that they had gathered, and the persons whom they had acquired in Haran; and they set forth to go to the land of Canaan.

Meditation

Hang on a minute, I said,
    let's get this straight:
    you're not serious, surely?

A trifle familiar, you might say,
    and you'd be right, I realise that now,
    but at the time I'd no idea who I was talking to,
    just this inner conviction
    that I should pick up sticks,
    head off to goodness knows where,
    and start again.
It was a lot to ask, wasn't it? –
    enough to make anyone in their right mind think twice.
Yet that's how it was for me,
    just this voice in my head
    telling me to pack my bags
    and head off into the wilderness,
    away to a land he would show me.
Was I simply restless, I wondered –
    the years bringing with them the urge to move on?
No, it wasn't that –
    deep down I knew, despite the doubts,
    that God was speaking to me –
    God as I'd never known him,
    never imagined him,
    never encountered him before.
And I was hooked, pure and simple,
    for here was a God unlike any other –
    mighty,
    majestic,
    mysterious –
    not *shaped* by our hands but *shaping* our lives,
    not *ours* to control but controlling *all*;
    a God beyond expression,
    sovereign over history,
    ruler over heaven and earth.
It was exhilarating and terrifying,
    a moment of promise, yet also of dread,
    for here was a call to leave home and livelihood,
    to tear up roots and forsake everything familiar –
    then venture out into the unknown.
Do you realise what that meant?
It wasn't just *me* involved, but my loved ones,
    them too asked to make the sacrifice
    and take the step of faith.
A lot to expect of anyone,
    even had we known the way ahead.

Yet they agreed,
    willingly,
    gladly,
    without a moment's hesitation,
    for they saw, so they told me,
    a light in my eyes
    and a flame in my heart,
    like nothing they'd seen before.
It was a hard journey,
    longer than we ever expected,
    with many a trial and tribulation along the way,
    but there were blessings too,
    surprises I could never have dreamt of,
    and the greatest of all
    is the lesson I've learned never to fear the future,
    for however uncertain it may be,
    and whatever it may bring,
    I realise now we must keep on travelling,
    journeying in faith,
    until our dying day.

To ponder

- He who hesitates is lost.
- The longer you look at it the less you will like it.
- Bold resolution is the favourite of providence.
- Opportunity seldom knocks twice.
- The first step is the hardest.
- Nothing ventured, nothing gained.
- He that stays in the valley shall never get over the hill.

To discuss

- We talk sometimes of faith being a journey into the unknown, but what does this mean? In what ways might God be asking this of you?
- Are you open to new insights, new ways of thinking and new experiences of God's love, or have you already decided where your journey of faith will take you?

To consider further

Read 2 Corinthians 4:16-18 and Hebrews 11:1-2, 8-16. Is God calling
you to step out in faith?

Prayer

Lord,
    you do not call us to a destination
    but a journey;
    a journey of continual new discoveries
    and new experiences of your love.
Save us from ever thinking we have arrived,
    from imagining we know all there is to know
    or that we have exhausted the riches
    of everything you would reveal to us.
Open our eyes to the great adventure of life
    and to the unfathomable mysteries of your purpose,
    and so help us to be a pilgrim people,
    travelling in faith as Abraham travelled before us,
    until we reach at last the kingdom
    you hold in store for all your people.
Amen.

6 Amazing grace _____

_____ *Abraham*

The story of Abraham and Isaac is one I have never found easy, for the very idea of sacrificing a child is utterly repellent. That Abraham could have contemplated it for a moment, even though he believed God had called him to it, seems hard to stomach. Yet to approach the incident in this way is almost certainly to miss the point. Not only does the passage serve to distinguish the Jewish faith from many religions of its time by rejecting human in favour of animal sacrifice; more importantly it points to faith that God would provide; a faith ultimately vindicated. Whether Abraham would ever have plunged the knife in we can never know – I like to think not. What we do know is that God removed the need; and not just *here* through a ram caught in a thicket, but *for ever* through a 'lamb' impaled on a cross.

Reading – Genesis 22:1-13

After these things God tested Abraham. He said to him, 'Abraham!' And he said, 'Here I am.' He said, 'Take your son, your only son Isaac, whom you love, and go to the land of Moriah, and offer him there as a burnt offering on one of the mountains that I shall show you.' So Abraham rose early in the morning, saddled his donkey, and took two of his young men with him, and his son Isaac; he cut the wood for the burnt offering, and set out and went to the place in the distance that God had shown him. On the third day Abraham looked up and saw the place far away. Then Abraham said to his young men, 'Stay here with the donkey; the boy and I will go over there; we will worship, and then we will come back to you. Abraham took the wood of the burnt offering and laid it on his son Isaac, and he himself carried the fire and the knife. So the two of them walked on together. Isaac said to his father Abraham, 'Father!' And he said, 'Here I am, my son.' He said, 'The fire and the wood are here, but where is the lamb for a burnt offering?' Abraham said, 'God himself will provide the lamb for a burnt offering, my son.' So the two of them walked on together.

When they came to the place that God had shown him, Abraham built an altar there and laid the wood in order. He bound his son Isaac, and laid him on the altar, on top of the wood. Then Abraham reached out his hand and took the knife to kill his son. The angel of the Lord

called to him from heaven, and said, 'Abraham, Abraham!' And he
said, 'Here I am.' He said, 'Do not lay your hand on the boy or do anything to him; for now I know that you fear God, since you have not
withheld your son, your only son, from me.' And Abraham looked up
and saw a ram, caught in a thicket by its horns. Abraham went and
took the ram and offered it up as a burnt offering instead of his son.

Meditation

Could I have gone through with it –
   slaughtered my son as a sacrifice to God?
If I'm honest, no,
    the very idea horrific,
    unimaginable!
I loved that boy more than my own self,
    the most precious thing in the world to me,
    and to think of plunging in the knife,
    watching the flames consume him –
    it was too much,
    more than I could ever bear.
So I shut the thought out,
    hoping and praying
    that when the moment of truth came
    God would call a halt,
    come up with something else I could sacrifice instead.
What if he hadn't, I hear you ask?
And the answer? –
    I think I'd have killed *myself*,
    for there was no way I could have lived with my conscience
    had I harmed the lad.
But it didn't come to that, God be praised –
    at the last moment a ram caught my eye,
    its horns caught in a thicket –
    and I knew that God had simply been testing me all along,
    measuring the depth of my devotion
    and the extent of my faith.
But I'll never forget that expression on my son's face –
    that heart-breaking mixture
    of fear, confusion and disbelief
    as I stood over him,
    knife poised,

sweat pouring from my brow,
    looking down with such dreadful anguish.
I think I was shaking more than him!
We laughed about it afterwards,
    made out it was all a joke,
    and thankfully he believed me –
    or wanted to anyway –
    but it took a long time
    before I could look him in the eye again.
And as for Sarah, I never breathed a word of it,
    nor Isaac either, thank God.
I passed the test though, so it seems,
    God having blessed me since more than I deserve.
Yet I know in my heart,
    as I'm sure he knows too,
    that though I love him dearly,
    with heart and soul and mind,
    I love my boy more.
I'm just grateful that, in his mercy, God understood,
    pushing me hard, but not beyond my limit,
    for let's face it, offering your love is one thing,
    but giving your own son to show it –
    surely nobody could love enough for that!

To ponder

- The grace of God is enough.
- Divine grace was never slow.
- God provides for him who trusts.
- He who serves God, serves a good master.

To discuss

- The point of this story is that it was God who provided the necessary sacrifice, not man. Have we taken that wonderful truth into our lives?
- Does God having taken the initiative mean there is nothing we must do on our part? If not, what is asked of us?

To consider further

Read Revelation 5:6-14. Rejoice in the fact that God has accomplished through his grace what we can never hope to achieve through our own efforts!

Prayer

Gracious God,
    you call us to a life of self-sacrifice,
    service and dedication to you.
Yet you know our weakness,
    and understand how hard we find it
    to offer even a little, let alone much.
We thank you that in your mercy
    you came to us through your only Son,
    the Word made flesh,
    and through him
    made the sacrifice we are incapable of making;
    an offering which alone can atone for our sin.
Gracious God,
    we praise you for your love which knows no bounds,
    which gave all
    so that we may receive life in all its fullness.
Receive our grateful worship,
    and consecrate our lives to your service.
Amen.

7 Pearls before swine? _____

_____ *Esau*

There are some stories which leave a bitter taste in the mouth, seeming to contradict everything we believe about right and wrong. For me, the epic saga of Esau and Jacob is one such example. It features a man who was to become one of the founding fathers of Judaism, revered ever since as one of the great servants of God. Yet if the outcome for Jacob was a happy one, for Esau it was anything but. Swindled out of his birthright through little apparent fault of his own, he was left to make the best of a thoroughly bad job. Those seeking reassuring spiritual truths from these pages beware, for they will find instead a concoction of treachery, self-interest and opportunism on a breathtaking scale. We sanitise these away at our peril. Esau was by no means perfect, but, morally speaking, compared with Jacob, he comes across as an angel. Yet it is Jacob who finally runs away with the spoils. Lessons certainly can be learned from these narratives but, like it or not, we are dealing here finally with the grace of God which confounds all our expectations. To face up to that truth is a profoundly disturbing experience.

Reading – Genesis 25:29-30; 27:30-38

Once when Jacob was cooking a stew, Esau came in from the field, and he was famished. Esau said to Jacob, 'Let me eat some of that red stuff, for I am famished!' . . . Jacob said, 'First sell me your birthright.' Esau said, 'I am about to die; of what use is a birthright to me?' Jacob said, 'Swear to me first.' So he swore to him, and sold his birthright to Jacob. Then Jacob gave Esau bread and lentil stew, and he ate and drank, and rose and went his way. Thus Esau despised his birthright . . .

(Some time later, Jacob, with the connivance of his mother, has successfully appropriated his father's blessing.)

As soon as Isaac had finished blessing Jacob, when Jacob had scarcely gone out from the presence of his father Isaac, his brother Esau came in from his hunting. He also prepared savoury food, and brought it to his father. And he said to his father, 'Let my father sit up and eat of his son's game, so that you may bless me.' His father Isaac said to him, 'Who are you?' He answered, 'I am your firstborn son, Esau.' Then Isaac trembled violently, and said, 'Who was it then that hunted game and brought it to me, and I ate it all before you came, and I have blessed him? – yes, and blessed he shall be!' When Esau heard his father's words, he cried out

with an exceedingly great and bitter cry, and said to his father, 'Bless me,
me also, father!' But he said, 'Your brother came deceitfully, and he has
taken away your blessing.' Esau said, 'Is he not rightly named Jacob? For
he has supplanted me these two times. He took away my birthright; and
look, now he has taken away my blessing.' Then he said, 'Have you not
reserved a blessing for me?' Isaac answered Esau, 'I have already made
him your lord, and I have given him all his brothers as servants, and
with grain and wine I have sustained him. What then can I do for you,
my son?' Esau said to his father, 'Have you only one blessing, father?
Bless me, me also, father!' And Esau lifted up his voice and wept.

Meditation

Let's face it, I was a complete fool.
It doesn't help much to admit it,
    for I still feel angry sometimes,
    even bitter –
    cheated so shamelessly out of my rightful inheritance –
    but I had it coming to me, it has to be said,
    victim finally of my own folly.
Yes, there was a certain naiveté, fair enough,
    a simple, almost childish, trust
    ruthlessly taken advantage of;
    but it ran deeper than that,
    exposing a lazy careless streak I could never conquer,
    hard though I tried.
You see, I had everything I could ever want –
    heir to my father's inheritance,
    security and prosperity guaranteed,
    and what did I do with it? –
    I threw it all away for a bowl of soup!
Talk about casting pearls before swine!
It was crass stupidity,
    unforgivable,
    but I was ravenous that morning,
    fit to drop,
    at the time filling my belly all that seemed to matter,
    so I traded away my birthright
    for a moment's fleeting satisfaction.
Exploited? Certainly!
And you may well call that brother of mine
    a devious twisted opportunist.
But he understood the things in life which really matter

more than I ever could;
   while I dwelt on my stomach
   he looked to the future,
   an eye for tomorrow as well as today.
I thought I'd undone the damage even then,
   that morning when Dad called me in
   and promised his blessing.
It was the chance I'd been looking for,
   and I raced off excitedly to prepare the meal he'd asked for,
   heart skipping,
   hope bubbling anew.
I should have noticed that look in Mother's eye,
   the thoughtful, scheming gleam,
   but I didn't;
   and while my back was turned, my brother nipped in,
   pulling the wool over my father's eyes
   with no sign of remorse.
It was a dastardly trick,
   just about finishing the poor fellow off,
   and when I learned the truth I was seething,
   intent only on revenge.
God knows, I'd have killed him given half the chance,
   torn him limb from limb without a shred of conscience,
   but he made himself scarce until my temper cooled,
   knowing full well I'd come round in time.
And I did, sure enough.
Call me a fool if you like,
   but when he slunk back to meet me all those years later,
   tail between his legs,
   I hadn't the heart to have a go at him;
   welcoming him instead like a long-lost brother.
Yes, it still rankles occasionally, even now –
   when I think what might have been,
   what I could have had,
   but, you see, it was mine for the taking,
   and I let it go,
   a priceless treasure allowed to slip through my fingers.
He wanted it most,
   and made it his,
   fixing his eyes not on a passing pleasure
   but an eternal promise,
   and much though it pains me to say it,
   that difference between us says it all.

To ponder

- He who wills the end, wills the means.
- The wish is father to the thought.
- We soon believe what we desire.
- If you deal with a fox, think of his tricks.
- Trust is the mother of deceit.
- Half the truth is often a whole lie.
- Poor by condition, rich by ambition.

To discuss

- Cheats never prosper, or so we are told. But is that true?
- How do you reconcile this story with the fact that Jacob secured the blessing of his father through a callous act of deception?
- Was Esau hard done by in this story, or was he the victim of his own stupidity?
- In what ways do we make the same mistake as Esau?

To consider further

Read Matthew 6:33-34. Ask yourself honestly what things are most important in your life? Have you got your priorities right?

Prayer

Lord,
　　you have given us so much to enjoy –
　　a world full of infinite variety and fascination.
We thank you for everything within it
　　that gives us pleasure,
　　that interests and excites us,
　　that fills our minds with wonder
　　and our hearts with joy.
Teach us to appreciate all you have given
　　and to celebrate accordingly.
But teach us also to recognise
　　those things in life which matter most of all,
　　which alone can satisfy not just the body
　　but also the soul.
Help us to crave your blessing
　　and hunger for your kingdom;
　　then give us the resolve we need
　　to reach out and make these ours.
Amen.

8 A life-changing experience

Jacob

It's a sad fact of life that few things live up to our expectations. We can spend years striving to reach some goal which we think will answer all our problems, only to find, no sooner do we achieve it, that we are overwhelmed by a sense of anticlimax. There is, I believe, something of this truth in the celebrated story of Jacob's dream at Bethel. For years he had plotted and schemed to swindle his brother Esau out of his rightful inheritance and, at last, with the connivance of his mother, the opportunity came. Yet after the initial flush of success, the inevitable questions surfaced. Exactly what went through his mind we can never know but I suspect it was along these lines: Was it all worth it? Surely there is more to life than material gain. In the vision that came to him that night, Jacob was to realise there is indeed more – far more than he'd ever begun to contemplate.

Reading – Genesis 28:10-17

Jacob left Beer-sheba and went toward Haran. He came to a certain place and stayed there for the night, because the sun had set. Taking one of the stones of the place, he put it under his head and lay down in that place. And he dreamed that there was a ladder set up on earth, the top of it reaching to heaven; and the angels of God were ascending and descending on it. And the Lord stood beside him and said, 'I am the Lord, the God of Abraham your father and the God of Isaac; the land on which you lie I will give to you and to your offspring; and your offspring shall be like the dust of the earth, and you shall spread abroad to the west and to the east and to the north and to the south; and all the families of the earth shall be blessed in you and in your offspring. Know that I am with you and will keep you wherever you go, and will bring you back to this land; for I will not leave you until I have done what I have promised you.' Then Jacob woke from his sleep and said, 'Surely the Lord is in this place – and I did not know it!' And he was afraid, and said, 'How awesome is this place! This is none other than the house of God, and this is the gate of heaven.'

Meditation

Have you ever been brought down to earth with a bump?
I was last night,
   and strangely enough
   by – of all things – a vision of heaven!
I was feeling so pleased with myself,
   so smug and self-satisfied,
   for I'd secured the future I'd always wanted,
   the inheritance of my dreams –
   or so I thought.
Only suddenly, as I lay on that makeshift pillow of mine,
   tossing and turning in fitful sleep,
   I realised it wasn't that simple,
   the awful truth hitting me
   that my trickery and treachery had all been in vain,
   for the blessing I'd so wantonly filched
   was as nothing beside the riches I glimpsed then,
   the blessing of God himself,
   the Lord of heaven and earth.
I'd given him little thought until then –
   faith pretty much academic,
   failing to touch the daily business of life –
   but in that astonishing vision I felt him close,
   challenging,
   confronting,
   calling me to account –
   an unexpected day of reckoning.
I'd believed I could control the future,
   shape my destiny,
   but now I saw I couldn't.
I'd imagined wealth and success spelt happiness,
   yet I understood suddenly that it wasn't true.
I'd thought I could act with impunity,
   never mind the consequences,
   only then the voice of conscience reared its head.
It was an eerie moment,
   exhilarating yet terrifying,
   bringing supreme joy and agonising humiliation,
   for I was suddenly naked before God,
   the folly of my actions,
   the smallness of my vision,
   laid bare,
   and life was changed for ever.

I was brought down to earth with a vengeance,
    everything I thought I'd achieved
    exposed for the illusion it was.
But I tell you this,
    I left that place rejoicing,
    spirit dancing within me,
    for I was touched by the sheer wonder of grace,
    and I met there the God who not only brings us low
    but who is able to lift us up
    to heights beyond our imagining.

To ponder

- God comes at last when we think he is farthest off.
- Man's extremity is God's opportunity.
- Man does what he can, and God does what he will.
- Step by step the ladder is ascended.

To discuss

- Recall past moments in your experience when moments of joy and triumph were followed by a sense of anticlimax. How do you explain those times? What sort of things went on in your mind?
- Can you recall times when you have been very conscious of God's presence? What was it that made him seem near?
- In what ways during your life have you been conscious of God's challenge, calling you to faith and repentance, or offering a new direction in life? What or who did God speak through, and how did you respond?

To consider further

Read Matthew 6:19-21, Luke 12:15-21 and 1 Peter 5:6-7. Are you pinning your hopes in life on some goal or dream which ultimately has no power to offer fulfilment? Have you the courage to be honest with yourself, and the humility to acknowledge your need so that God can respond to it?

Prayer

Living God,
    so often we spend our lives
    chasing after empty dreams with no power to satisfy.
We allow ourselves to be swallowed up
    by the material and trivial,
    and all the time our souls ache within us,
    crying out for life-giving water.
Help us to catch sight of your kingdom,
    to glimpse your glory,
    to hunger and thirst after righteousness.
Bring us low,
    that through your grace we might rise high.
Amen.

9 Do as you would be done by _____

_____ *Rachel*

Crime, we are told, doesn't pay. Or, to put it another way, your sins will find you out. But is that true? It's hard sometimes, when greed and corruption seem to prosper all around us, not to feel that we've got it wrong, such fine-sounding maxims a shade too simplistic for this rough old world of ours. And, on the surface, the saga of Jacob does nothing to allay that feeling; if anything serving only to compound it. Yet if we dig deeper, a different picture emerges. It's not that Jacob gets his comeuppance – to say that would be stretching things too far – but as the story unfolds there are at least signs that some kind of accountability exists in this life. The measure we give is ultimately the measure we get. Through a mixture of cunning and deceit Jacob undeniably secured great rewards for himself. But he was to find that two can play the same game, and the consequences could hardly have been more fitting.

Reading – Genesis 29:16-23, 25-28, 30

Now Laban had two daughters; the name of the elder was Leah, and the name of the younger was Rachel. Leah's eyes were lovely, and Rachel was graceful and beautiful. Jacob loved Rachel; so he said, 'I will serve you seven years for your younger daughter Rachel.' Laban said, 'It is better that I should give her to you than that I should give her to any other man; stay with me.' So Jacob served seven years for Rachel, and they seemed to him but a few days because of the love he had for her. Then Jacob said to Laban, 'Give me my wife that I may go in to her, for my time is completed.' So Laban gathered together all the people of the place, and made a feast. But in the evening he took his daughter Leah and brought her to Jacob; and he went in to her.

When morning came, it was Leah! And Jacob said to Laban, 'What is this you have done to me? Did I not serve with you for Rachel? Why then have you deceived me? Laban said, 'This is not done in our country – giving the younger before the firstborn. Complete the week of this one, and we will give you the other also in return for serving me another seven years.' Jacob did so, and completed her week; then Laban gave him his daughter Rachel as a wife.

So Jacob went in to Rachel also, and he loved Rachel more than Leah. He served Laban for another seven years.

Meditation

He was livid when he found out,
    more angry than I have ever known him,
    and with good cause.
It was a shabby trick they played –
    one that could have destroyed all our futures,
    not just mine –
    and when I realised what they were up to
    I was beside myself,
    begging them to think again, though to no avail.
Poor Jacob, what a shock it must have been,
    to wake up that morning –
    head still throbbing from the night before –
    to find my sister there instead of me.
And poor Leah,
    to see that look of fury,
    disgust,
    disappointment on his face,
    more eloquent and damning than words could ever be.
She loved him, you see,
    as much as I did,
    worshipping the very ground he walked on,
    so when the plot was hatched
    she couldn't believe her luck –
    it was like a dream come true.
I felt sorry for her later, I really did,
    for she'd have done anything for just one of his smiles,
    a word of affection,
    a peck on the cheek;
    but it was me he wanted, all too clearly,
    and at the time it was Jacob my heart bled for,
    so cruelly and wickedly deceived.
Seven years he'd worked for me,
    seven long years of unmitigated slog –
    my father a hard taskmaster, kinsman or no kinsman –
    but he did it willingly,
    an act of devotion,
    longing for that moment when we could be together,
    husband and wife at last.
It was snatched from his grasp,
    and I dreaded the consequences,
    petrified he might walk away,
    our dream destroyed for ever.

But he didn't;
    he promised to stay,
    just as my father had bargained on,
    seven more years' hard graft to make me his –
    could any girl ask for more?
He was bitter afterwards, understandably,
    determined to exact revenge,
    and I couldn't blame him,
    for I felt hurt myself.
But do you know what? A funny thing happened yesterday.
We were together, just the two of us,
    talking about old times,
    and I happened to mention that fateful night,
    his being taken in like that –
    duped into mistaking Leah for me –
    and then swallowing that feeble excuse
    about the firstborn deserving their rights.
I was only teasing him,
    just a bit of harmless fun really,
    but suddenly Jacob looked at me,
    a look of wonder and comprehension in his eyes,
    as though a light had dawned,
    a mystery been unravelled,
    and the next moment he threw back his head,
    and laughed till the tears rolled down his face.
He saw a joke somewhere that I'd never intended,
    a sense in which God was having the last laugh.
Can you see it?
I wish I could.

To ponder

- To deceive a deceiver is no deceit.
- Who thinks to deceive God has already deceived himself.
- One lie makes many.
- Experience is the best teacher.
- No marvel if the imps follow where the devil goes before.

To discuss

- Do you think that God was teaching Jacob a lesson through this story, or is it more a question of Jacob reaping what he sowed?

- Everyone in this story paid some kind of price. For whom do you think the cost was greatest, and why?
- How true is it that the consequences of our actions always finally catch up with us? What is the best way of dealing with our mistakes?

To consider further

Read Luke 6:37-38 and Galatians 6:7-10. How far do these words sum up the experience of Jacob?

Prayer

Lord,
    there are times when life doesn't seem fair,
    when those who openly flout your will
    seem to prosper,
    while those who follow you
    gain scant reward.
We know this shouldn't matter to us –
    that our treasure should be in heaven
    rather than on earth,
    our hearts set on things eternal
    rather than the riches of this world –
    yet it's hard sometimes not to feel frustrated,
    even resentful,
    at the apparent injustice of life.
Forgive us the times we have made that mistake,
    setting ourselves up as judge and jury.
Forgive us the times we have doubted you in consequence,
    questioning your justice and resenting your grace.
Teach us to understand that, whoever we are,
    our actions will finally catch up with us,
    and so help us to live faithfully as your people,
    rejoicing in the blessings you have given,
    and anticipating the joy yet to come.
Amen.

10 Grappling with God _____

_____ *Jacob*

Grappling with God – it's a strange idea, isn't it? Very different from the more traditional picture of humble and obedient acceptance. Yet that is what we find in surely one of the most dramatic if enigmatic incidents recorded anywhere in the Bible. The imagery is crude, if not shocking – a mysterious stranger who accosts Jacob by the ford at Jabbok turning out to be none other than God himself. More puzzling still, so tenaciously does Jacob cling hold during the ensuing test of strength that God is unable to extricate himself without first granting a blessing. It all gets, as Alice might have said, 'curiouser and curiouser'. Yet it is the very primitiveness of this encounter which for me is so compelling. There is no false piety here, no alabaster saint as far removed from our human condition as it is possible to be. Here is an individual like you or me, coming warts and all before God and struggling to come to terms with the complex realities of life and faith. Who knows quite what Jacob wrestled with in the darkness of that night – doubt, fear, pride, guilt? – you name it and it was probably there! Symbolic the whole story may be but its power remains undiminished, giving hope and encouragement to all those like me who grapple with God in their turn.

Reading – Genesis 32:9-12, 22-31

Jacob said, 'O God of my father Abraham and God of my father Isaac, O Lord who said to me, "Return to your country and to your kindred, and I will do you good", I am not worthy of the least of all the stead-fast love and all the faithfulness that you have shown to your servant, for with only my staff I crossed this Jordan; and now I have become two companies. Deliver me, please, from the hand of my brother, from the hand of Esau, for I am afraid of him; he may come and kill us all, the mothers with the children. Yet you have said, "I will surely do you good, and make your offspring as the sand of the sea, which cannot be counted because of their number".'

The same night he got up and took his two wives, his two maids, and his eleven children, and crossed the ford of Jabbok. He took them and sent them across the stream, and likewise everything that he had. Jacob was left alone; and a man wrestled with him until daybreak. When the man saw that he did not prevail against Jacob, he struck him on the hip socket, and Jacob's hip was put out of joint as he wrestled with him. Then he said, 'Let me go, for the day is breaking.' But Jacob said, 'I will not let you go, unless you bless me.' So he said to him, 'What is your name?' And he said, 'Jacob.' Then the man said, 'You shall no longer be called Jacob, but Israel, for you have striven with God and with humans, and have prevailed.' Then Jacob asked him, 'Please tell me your name.' But he said, 'Why is it that you ask my name?' And there he blessed him. So Jacob called the place Penuel, saying, 'For I have seen God face to face, and yet my life is preserved.' The sun rose upon him as he passed Penuel, limping because of his hip.

Meditation

There was no way I deserved it,
    no reason God should have blessed me.
I was under no illusions about that,
    no false sense of my own worthiness.
I was a two-faced, scheming swindler,
    and I knew it as well as any,
    but if that was down to me it was also down to God,
    for he made me that way,
    the responsibility at least his in part.
So I reckoned he owed me something –
    a place in his purpose,
    a share in his promise.
Only it cut both ways,
    for he reckoned *I* owed *him* something too –
    obedience,
    worship,
    faith.
And the result was inevitable –
    somewhere,
    some time,
    we had to clash,
    thrash the whole business out,
    sort out once and for all exactly where we stood.
And that's what happened,
    one dark night by the ford of Jabbok,
    a night I shall never forget as long as I live.
Did it really happen as I remember it?
I can't be sure.
Perhaps it was just a dream,

perhaps a vision,
perhaps simply a crisis of conscience,
but suddenly this stranger blocked my path,
daring me to pass –
and we were locked in mortal combat,
wrestling for grim death as the hours ticked away.
Did I defeat him?
I thought so at the time,
refusing to let him go until he blessed me,
but I realised later he could have destroyed me
had he wished,
tossed me aside with a flick of the wrist.
He was testing my resolve,
assessing my commitment,
measuring my determination to grasp the future
come what may;
and if I was willing to play my part, he'd play his.
I knew for sure then what I'd suspected all along –
I'd been grappling with God,
and myself,
wrestling with my inner doubts and hidden fears,
struggling with my stubborn greed,
my troubled mind, my aching soul.
I could have backed away, of course,
turned aside and ignored the challenge,
but the time for running was over –
I was on the spot,
face to face with God,
face to face with self –
a time to decide.
It changed my life, that moment,
a new beginning from which I never looked back.
Yes, the encounter was bruising,
but it brought me a wholeness I have never known before,
impossible to describe –
an inner health of body, mind and spirit –
whole, at last!

To ponder

- Have at it, and have it.
- He begins to die that quits his desires.

- He conquers, who endures.
- If at first you don't succeed, try, try, try again.
- He who rides a tiger is afraid to dismount.

To discuss

- Who or what do you think Jacob was grappling with in his encounter with God: himself, God, or the realities of life?
- Which of the above do you find hardest to face honestly?
- Is it right that we have to wrestle with God? In what ways?

To consider further

Read Acts 26:9-18, Philippians 2:12-13 and Hebrews 4:11-13. Are there areas in your life where you are fighting against God?

Prayer

Gracious God,
    you created us in your image
    to enjoy a living relationship with you.
And though we fail you time and again,
    you continually reach out to us,
      longing to break down the barriers which keep us apart
      so that you can call us your children.
We have no claim on your love,
    no reason to feel we deserve it,
      for we are false and faithless in so much.
Forgive us for sometimes forgetting that truth,
    imagining that we are better than we really are.
Teach us to face ourselves openly and honestly,
    to wrestle with the harsh realities of life
    and the vast mysteries of faith;
    and, above all, teach us to recognise
    our dependence on your divine grace.
Amen.

11 The folly of favouritism _____

_____ *Jacob*

According to the words of an old saying, you can't bury the past. For Jacob, or rather Israel as he had become called, the truth of those words must have seemed all too real as his sons returned from the fields with the shattering news that his son Joseph was dead! Illogical though it may be, there seems to be an instinctive human tendency to interpret any kind of misfortune in terms of divine retribution, and I've no doubt Jacob did much the same, his mind instinctively harking back to his all too murky past. Yet while such a view of God undoubtedly finds a place in the Old Testament, so also does a very different picture; the portrayal of a God always willing to forgive and forget, ready to put the past behind us, however little we may deserve it, so that we may begin again. This is the God, fortunately for him, who emerges time and again in the story of Jacob – the God who we see most fully revealed in the person of Christ.

Reading – Genesis 37:3-4, 12-13a, 14, 17b-20, 22-24a, 26-28, 31-35

Now Israel loved Joseph more than any other of his children, because he was the son of his old age; and he had made him a long robe with sleeves. But when his brothers saw that their father loved him more than all his brothers, they hated him, and could not speak peaceably to him.

Now his brothers went to pasture their father's flock near Shechem. And Israel said to Joseph, 'Go now, see if it is well with your brothers and with the flock; and bring word back to me.'

So Joseph went after his brothers, and found them at Dothan. They saw him from a distance, and before he came near to them, they conspired to kill him. They said to one another, 'Here comes this dreamer. Come now, let us kill him and throw him into one of the pits; then we shall say that a wild animal has devoured him, and we shall see what will become of his dreams.'

Reuben said to them, 'Shed no blood; throw him into this pit here in the wilderness, but lay no hand on him' – that he might rescue him out of their hand and restore him to their father. So when Joseph came to his brothers, they stripped him of his robe, the long robe with sleeves that he wore; and they took him and threw him into a pit.

Then Judah said to his brothers, 'What profit is it if we kill our brother and conceal his blood? Come, let us sell him to the Ishmaelites, and not lay our hands on him, for he is our brother, our own flesh.' And his

brothers agreed. When some Midianite traders passed by, they drew
Joseph up, lifting him up out of the pit, and sold him to the Ishmaelites
for twenty pieces of silver. And they took Joseph to Egypt.

Then they took Joseph's robe, slaughtered a goat, and dipped the
robe in the blood. They had the long robe with sleeves taken to their
father, and they said, 'This we have found; see now whether it is your
son's robe or not.' He recognised it, and said, 'It is my son's robe! A
wild animal has devoured him; Joseph is without doubt torn to pieces.'
Then Jacob tore his garments, and put sackcloth on his loins, and
mourned for his son many days. All his sons and all his daughters
sought to comfort him; but he refused to be comforted, and said, 'No,
I shall go down to Sheol to my son, mourning.'

Meditation

Was it a punishment for those mistakes long ago –
    God paying me back
    for having cheated and connived
    to make his blessing mine?
I thought so at the time,
    when my boys came back, all bar Joseph,
    heads bowed low,
    tears streaming down their faces,
    wringing their hands in sorrow.
I believed the worst at once,
    heart lurching within me.
Call me gullible, if you like,
    but what reason did I have to doubt their word?
They produced his robe, remember,
    dripping in blood,
    ripped to shreds,
    and I assumed immediately he'd been torn to pieces,
    my precious boy set upon by a wild beast.
All right, so they'd had their disagreements,
    even come to blows occasionally,
    but which boys don't? –
    it's a part of growing up.
They must have known he was harmless,
    despite those crazy dreams of his;
    conceited, perhaps,
    but innocent enough beneath it all.
I never dreamt for a moment they hated him,
    still less that they might do him in,
    so when they broke the news

I accepted it without question –
shattered,
inconsolable,
yet convinced it was true.
Divine judgement, it seemed, had come at last.
Only it wasn't God I should have blamed,
nor his brothers, come to that –
it was me,
for I was the cause of it all.
I spoiled him, you see, that lad of mine,
from the day he was born,
thrusting him forward,
pandering to his whims,
not just accepting his airs and graces,
but in many ways positively encouraging them.
Can you believe that? –
me of all people to make such a mistake,
after Father had doted on Esau
and Mother had time only for me!
It had torn us apart, their favouritism,
the seeds they sowed bearing terrible fruit,
and they'd died of a broken heart, the pair of them,
grieving for what might have been.
I should have learned from that,
remembered the bitterness and anger it caused,
and the dreadful steps it drove me to.
But I was blind,
and the wheel turned full circle.
It was fitting, I realised afterwards,
that I should be deceived in turn,
hoist, you might say, by my own petard,
but I couldn't have argued had the lad been dead,
for I deserved punishment after everything I'd done,
no sentence too severe.
Yet God was gracious.
his hand upon Joseph,
upon us all,
and I realise now that though in a sense
the past *did* catch up with me that day –
so much heartache of my own making –
it wasn't the past God was thinking of,
not for a moment,
but the future!

To ponder

- A guilty conscience needs no accuser.
- A man who has committed a mistake and doesn't correct it is committing another mistake. (*Confucius*)
- What's done cannot be undone. (*William Shakespeare*)
- There's no use crying over spilt milk.

To discuss

- Instead of learning from his father's mistakes, Jacob showed as much favouritism for Joseph as his father had shown for Isaac. Can you offer any explanation as to why this should have been?
- Are we any better at learning from the past than Jacob was?
- How often are we guilty of blaming God for situations which are ultimately of our own making?

To consider further

Read Matthew 7:1-5. Are we guilty of making the same mistakes which we condemn in others? Take time to look honestly at your life and assess where perhaps lessons need to be relearned.

Prayer

Lord,
    we find it hard to escape from the past.
It has shaped our lives in so many ways,
    helping to make us what we are today.
And though there have been successes,
    there have been mistakes also,
    too many of which continue to haunt us.
We find it hard to let go of regrets,
    hard to forgive,
    hardest of all to put past failures behind us
    and start again.
Yet you are the God who holds the future,
    always ready to forget what has been
    and lead us on to what shall be.
You are a God of new beginnings,
    new hope, new life.
Help us to grasp the full implications of what that means,
    and so help us to accept each day you give us
    and live it to the full,
    secure in the knowledge of your unfailing love.
Amen.

12 Resisting temptation

Joseph

Temptation comes in many shapes and forms. For some it is sex, for others money; for some drugs, for others power. All of us have our Achilles' heel – a vulnerable spot where temptation unerringly strikes – and though we may resist for a time it is hard not to succumb faced by temptation's repeated assaults. The same must have been true for Joseph, faced by the flirtatious advances of Potiphar's wife – he would have been less than human had he felt no stirring within him. Yet however attracted he may have been, he did not succumb, because he believed to do so would be to compromise everything he believed. Sold into slavery he may have been, rejected by his own brothers, and faced with an uncertain future in a foreign land; it didn't matter – the principles which underpinned his life and the faith which sustained these still held good. For Joseph, the all important factor was not what *he* desired but what *God* required. Here, quite simply, is the key to triumph over temptation.

Reading – Genesis 39:6b-20

Now Joseph was handsome and good-looking. And after a time his master's wife cast her eyes on Joseph and said, 'Lie with me.' But he refused and said to his master's wife, 'Look, with me here, my master has no concern about anything in the house, and he has put every-thing that he has in my hand. He is not greater in this house than I am, nor has he kept back anything from me except yourself, because you are his wife. How then could I do this great wickedness, and sin against God?' And although she spoke to Joseph day after day, he would not consent to lie beside her or to be with her. One day, however, when he went into the house to do his work, and while no one else was in the house, she caught hold of his garment, saying, 'Lie with me!' But he left his garment in her hand, and fled and ran outside. When she saw that he had left his garment in her hand and had fled outside, she called out to the members of her household and said to them, 'See, my husband has brought among us a Hebrew to insult us! He came in to me to lie with me, and I cried out with a loud voice; and when he heard me raise my voice and cry out, he left his garment beside me and fled outside.' Then she kept his garment by her until his master came home, and she told him the same story, saying, 'The Hebrew servant, whom you have brought among us, came in to me to insult me; but as soon as I raised my voice and cried out, he left his garment beside me, and fled outside.'

When his master heard the words that his wife spoke to him, saying, 'This is the way your servant treated me,' he became enraged. And Joseph's master took him and put him into the prison, the place where the king's prisoners were confined; he remained there in prison.

Meditation

Was I tempted? You bet I was!
She was an attractive woman, let's face it,
    suave,
    sophisticated,
    sexy,
    and I was a young man in my prime,
    flattered and excited by her attentions.
I felt my pulse racing when she looked at me,
    my palms sweating with anticipation,
    and I could have yielded so easily,
    my body crying out to surrender.
But I couldn't, despite myself,
    for both our sakes, not just mine.
Oh, I'd have enjoyed it, no doubt,
    for a moment, in the heat of passion,
    nothing else seeming to matter;
    but then the guilt would have started,
    the regrets,
    the sordid subterfuge,
    and finally, punishment!
She was married, you see,
    my master's wife,
    and the vows she'd taken were sacred,
    whichever god she'd made them by.
So I refused her, time and again,
    keeping my distance whenever I could.
Only she wouldn't take no for an answer,
    waiting patiently to seize her chance.
I should have it seen it coming, I suppose,
    for I knew she was put out –

you could see that a mile off –
  unused, apparently, to being turned down,
  but I never thought she'd come on that strong,
  not after all I'd said.
It was a close call eventually,
  too close for comfort,
  costing me my clothes, if not my virtue.
And it wasn't just my clothes I lost that day;
  it was my freedom,
  my position,
  my reputation,
  for she turned the tables as I knew she would,
  making *me* out to be the guilty party –
  'hell hath no fury . . .' as they say.
But whatever I lost, I kept far more,
  my integrity,
  my self-respect,
  and, above all, my faith.
A price worth paying, wouldn't you say?

To ponder

- A libertine life is not a life of liberty.
- Short pleasure, long repentance.
- The end of passion is the beginning of repentance.
- Fly that pleasure which pains afterwards.

To discuss

- Who would Joseph have let down most had he succumbed to the sexual advances made towards him; Potiphar, Potiphar's wife, himself or God? Why?
- What would have been the consequences for Joseph and Potiphar's wife had Joseph given in to temptation, even assuming no one found out about it?
- Why is sexual temptation so powerful?
- Are sexual misdemeanours any worse than others?

To consider further

Read 1 Corinthians 10:9-13 and Hebrews 4:14-16. Remind yourself of these verses next time temptation strikes.

Prayer

Loving God,
    you know what it is to be tempted,
    for you took on human flesh,
    making yourself frail and vulnerable,
    just as we are.
You know what it is to lose everything,
    for you gave your only Son
    for the life of the world.
For our sakes you became poor,
    enduring humiliation,
    yet you stood firm,
    refusing to be swayed
    or to contemplate compromise.
Teach us, in our turn,
    to hold fast, come what may.
When temptation comes,
    help us to look to you rather than self,
    to *your* kingdom rather than *our* gratification.
Show us the way you would have us take,
    and help us to walk it faithfully,
    now and always.
Amen.

13 Learning to forgive _____

_____ *Joseph*

There's no getting away from it – life is a strange paradox. At times it all goes smoothly, bringing joy and fulfilment, but at others it brings tragedy and sorrow, leaving us searching for answers, hopelessly bewildered as everything we put our trust in is turned upside down. How do we make sense of it? Can faith offer a solution? There are some who believe everything is planned by God down to the very last detail. They may be right, but personally I believe the answer is more complex – that God constantly needs to adapt his plans as time and again they are frustrated. Yet, as the story of Joseph reminds us, though life may be impossible to understand at the time, when we come to look back we can often discern God's hand at work, taking even the most terrible of moments and weaving them into his sovereign purpose.

Reading – Genesis 42:6-9, 15-16a, 21, 23-24a; 45:1-3, 14-15

Now Joseph was governor over the land; it was he who sold to all the people of the land. And Joseph's brothers came and bowed themselves before him with their faces to the ground. When Joseph saw his brothers, he recognised them, but he treated them like strangers and spoke harshly to them. 'Where do you come from?' he said. They said, 'From the land of Canaan, to buy food.' Although Joseph had recognised his brothers, they did not recognise him. Joseph also remembered the dreams that he had dreamed about them. He said to them, 'You are spies; you have come to see the nakedness of the land. . . . Here is how you shall be tested: as Pharaoh lives, you shall not leave this place unless your youngest brother comes here! Let one of you go and bring your brother, while the rest of you remain in prison, in order that your words may be tested . . .'

They said to one another, 'Alas, we are paying the penalty for what we did to our brother; we saw his anguish when he pleaded with us, but we would not listen. That is why this anguish has come upon us.' They did not know that Joseph understood them, since he spoke with them through an interpreter. He turned away from them and wept . . .

(Later, on their way home to Israel a second time, having returned once again to Egypt as the famine in Israel intensified, the twelve brothers were placed

under arrest as a cup which Joseph had secretly ordered to be planted there was found in Benjamin's sack. Grovelling before Joseph in terror, they pleaded for mercy, begging him to spare Benjamin, their father's favourite son, and offering to stand in his place if necessary.)

Then Joseph could no longer control himself before all those who stood by him, and he cried out, 'Send everyone away from me.' So no one stayed with him when Joseph made himself known to his brothers. And he wept so loudly that the Egyptians heard it, and the household of Pharaoh heard it. Joseph said to his brothers, 'I am Joseph. Is my father still alive?' But his brothers could not answer him, so dismayed were they at his presence.

Then he fell upon his brother Benjamin's neck and wept. And he kissed all his brothers and wept upon them; and after that his brothers talked with him.

Meditation

It couldn't be, I told myself –
    not here in Egypt,
    not my long-lost brothers,
    surely!
But it was!
Believe it or not, there they were,
    kneeling before me,
    prostrating themselves in homage.
It was astonishing,
    heart-rending,
    and it was all I could do not to break down in tears,
    such was the poignancy of the moment.
Only I couldn't, not yet,
    not after all they'd put me through.
Can you imagine what it was like,
    your own brothers plotting to kill you?
And then, sensing a reprieve, only to be sold into slavery,
    condemned to years of servitude
    in a strange and distant land.
I wasn't blameless, I knew that.
God knows, I'd given cause enough for resentment
    with those dreams of mine –
    even if they *were* coming true
    then and there before my eyes.
But though I could understand what they did, and why,
    I could never excuse it,

not a betrayal as vile as that.
So, you see, I had to test them,
    see if they'd learned their lesson
    or were still the same.
I made them sweat, to put it mildly,
    their hunted expression as I quizzed them saying it all;
    and when that cup turned up in Benjamin's sack,
    you should have seen their faces –
    it was as though their world had collapsed in pieces.
There seemed little doubt after that,
    their sincerity plain to all.
But I had to be sure,
    so I strung them along further,
    tormenting,
    teasing,
    until the perspiration poured off them
    and they begged for mercy.
It was my father's name which did it –
    when they spoke of him and all he'd suffered.
I broke down then,
    all the pain of those long and lonely years apart flooding out;
    and as the truth slowly dawned on them,
    breaking through their guilt,
    we held each other close,
    laughter mingling with tears,
    old feuds forgotten.
Was that the way it had to be,
    the way God planned it?
It's hard to believe –
    too many questions left unanswered –
    yet I tell you this,
    it wasn't just my brothers I found changed that day,
    it was me as much as any of them,
    each of us stronger and wiser for all we'd faced.
Suddenly life was sweeter and richer
    than we had ever imagined,
    as though somehow, despite everything we'd faced,
    it all made sense!

To ponder

- All's well that ends well.
- The noblest vengeance is to forgive.

- He who forgives others, God forgives him.
- Mercy surpasses justice.
- Forgiveness is perfect when the sin is not remembered. *(Arabic proverb)*

To discuss

- Feuds and grudges all too easily spring up out of the most innocent-looking disputes. What is essential if the damage caused by these is to be put right?
- What is the hardest thing about saying sorry, and the hardest thing in believing an apology to be genuine? What sort of barriers must be overcome on both sides?
- Many people are held captive by their past, unable to let bygones be bygones and move forward. What does the story of Joseph and his brothers have to say about avoiding such a danger?

To consider further

Read Matthew 6:12, Luke 17:3-4 and Mark 11:25. Is there somebody you need to forgive? Is it time perhaps you gave somebody who has let you down another chance?

Prayer

Lord,
  so often we don't understand what is happening to us.
We are swept along by a tide of circumstances,
    and we look in vain to find any pattern
    which might give meaning to it all.
This fleeting span of ours is a confusing riddle
    from which you can seem painfully absent.
Yet you are there even though we cannot see you,
    patiently weaving the broken strands of life
    into an intricate tapestry.
Teach us, then, to trust in you and live by faith
    until that day when the picture is complete
    and we understand at last
    all the ways you have been working
    to bring order out of chaos.
Amen.

14 The price of prejudice

A Hebrew slave

Last week I saw a documentary about the Jewish Holocaust in Nazi Germany. It wasn't the first time I'd seen pictures of those dreadful years, but, as ever, they left me numbed, shocked, horrified. To be confronted with such stark atrocities, such appalling suffering, forces a reappraisal of life and re-evaluation of faith, for how can we ever begin to reconcile such unadulterated evil with a God of love? I have no easy answers, only the humbling knowledge that many Jews continue today, despite all they have been through, to believe passionately in the enduring purpose of God for their nation. Faith somehow lives with mystery, even contradiction, refusing to be snuffed out. We may imagine that the Holocaust was a one-off aberration, a never to be repeated act of lunacy. History warns otherwise – its pages littered with xenophobia, ethnic cleansing and mass genocide. None of us can afford to forget the terrible consequences to which prejudice can lead; prejudice which lurks deep in every one of us. Of all people, the Jewish nation understands what the awful human cost can be.

Reading – Exodus 1:8-16

Now a new king arose over Egypt, who did not know Joseph. He said to his people, 'Look, the Israelite people are more numerous and more powerful than we. Come, let us deal shrewdly with them, or they will increase and, in the event of war, join our enemies and fight against us and escape from the land.' Therefore they set taskmasters over them to oppress them with forced labour. They built supply cities, Pithom and Rameses, for Pharaoh. But the more they were oppressed, the more they multiplied and spread, so that the Egyptians came to dread the Israelites. The Egyptians became ruthless in imposing tasks on the Israelites, and made their lives bitter with hard service in mortar and brick and in every kind of field labour. They were ruthless in all the tasks that they imposed on them.

The king of Egypt said to the Hebrew midwives, one of them named Shiphrah and the other Puah, 'When you act as midwives to the Hebrew women, and see them on the birthstool, if it is a boy, kill him; but if it is a girl, she shall live.'

Meditation

They hated us –
   not because we'd done wrong,
   nor through any fault on our part,
   but because we were different –
   another culture,
   another faith,
   another race.
It was as simple as that.
Immigrants, they called us – and worse;
   good-for-nothing layabouts, sponging off their state,
   stealing their women,
   taking their jobs,
   sapping their wealth,
   spoiling their country.
It was nonsense, of course, everybody knew it –
   we'd become part of their land,
   our lives and destiny interwoven;
   pursuing our own faith, admittedly,
   worshipping our own God,
   but loyal, law-abiding citizens.
Oh yes, they knew,
   but they preferred to forget it,
   for they wanted someone to blame for their troubles –
   someone to hound,
   someone to hate,
   someone to hurt –
   and we were the ones chosen,
   the luckless scapegoats herded off for sacrifice.
What did they do to us? You wouldn't believe it.
Things too unspeakable, too terrible to mention!
Yet they were people, that's what I can't understand,
   ordinary people like you or me;
   folk we'd walked with, talked with,
   worked with, laughed with,
   suddenly cruel, cold, callous monsters.
One day we were human,
   the next, objects;
   one day, friend,
   the next, foe.
Who'd have believed things could change so quickly,
   the world turn upside down?
We were different, that's all,

another tongue,
another creed,
but, for all that, we were still people, just as they were,
flesh and blood feeling joy and sorrow, pleasure and pain.
I thought that mattered,
that whatever divided us, more must unite,
but I was wrong,
so hideously, hopelessly wrong.
Was God to blame?
I believed so at the time,
asking myself, day after day,
how he could stand by and let it happen,
remote in heaven from such dreadful crimes on earth.
And it troubled me deeply,
as much as the suffering itself,
my faith shaken,
dangling on a thread.
But it wasn't God, I realise that now –
it was man,
man as I never dreamt he could be;
one human being destroying another,
life counting for nothing –
and that disturbs me yet more.

To ponder

- We are all Adam's children.
- All bloods are alike ancient.
- Beauty is only skin deep.
- It is profound ignorance that inspires the dogmatic tone.

To discuss

- A holocaust couldn't happen today, or could it? Recent events in Bosnia and Kosovo show all too clearly that ethnic hatred is still very much alive. What are the causes of racism and other forms of discrimination, and how, if at all, can these be overcome?
- Religious prejudice has led to more hatred and suffering than any other form of prejudice. Is this true, and, if so, can anything be done to prevent it happening again in the future?

- Can Christianity enter into dialogue with other faiths yet remain true to itself?

To consider further

Read John 1:43-46 and James 2:1-9. In what ways does prejudice and discrimination still have a hold in your life? Think about it honestly before rushing to answer.

Prayer

Lord,
    you have made us all different,
    with different characters, different gifts,
    different opinions, different insights.
Yet you have made us also, every one of us,
    in your own image,
    uniquely precious to you.
Forgive us that we allow our differences to come between us
    rather than draw us together;
    that we see them as a threat rather than a gift.
Forgive us that we find it so hard to change.
We do our best to overcome the prejudice within us,
    but it runs deep,
    emerging in ways we fail to recognise,
    poisoning our very souls.
Teach us to look at ourselves and others with your eyes,
    seeing the good and the bad,
    the lovely and the unlovely,
    the strengths and the weaknesses,
    the truths and the falsehoods,
    yet seeing always our common humanity.
Open our hearts and minds to one another,
    and so also to you.
Amen.

15 Rising to the challenge

Moses

When were you last confronted with a challenge which seemed completely beyond you but which somehow you had to face? Anyone who has been in such a situation will have some insight into how Moses must have felt when God unexpectedly called him to go before Pharaoh in Egypt and demand the release of his people. It was a lot to ask of anyone, but for someone like Moses, nervous and hesitant in speech, it was little short of purgatory. This was one request he could do without! The trouble was, God apparently couldn't do without *him*. And so began one of the most astonishing conversations between God and man recorded in Scripture. On the one hand we have the sheer humanity of Moses, coming up with reason after reason why he's the least suitable candidate for the job, and on the other we find God countering every argument with an unanswerable riposte. It's hard not to feel sorry for Moses as finally he is almost browbeaten into submission. But it is impossible equally not to be inspired by the God who provides all the resources needed, and more besides, to face the challenge he brings.

Reading – Exodus 3:1-15

Moses was keeping the flock of his father-in-law Jethro, the priest of Midian; he led his flock beyond the wilderness, and came to Horeb, the mountain of God. There the angel of the Lord appeared to him in a flame of fire out of a bush; he looked and the bush was blazing, yet it was not consumed. Then Moses said, 'I must turn aside and look at this great sight, and see why the bush is not burned up.' When the Lord saw that he had turned aside to see, God called to him out of the bush, 'Moses, Moses!' And he said, 'Here I am.' Then he said, 'Come no closer! Remove the sandals from your feet, for the place on which you are standing is holy ground.' He said further, 'I am the God of your father, the God of Abraham, the God of Isaac, and the God of Jacob.' And Moses hid his face, for he was afraid to look at God.

Then the Lord said, 'I have observed the misery of my people who are in Egypt; I have heard their cry on account of their taskmasters. Indeed, I know their sufferings, and I have come down to deliver them from the Egyptians, and to bring them up out of that land to a good and broad land, a land flowing with milk and honey, to the country of the Canaanites, the Hittites, the Amorites, the Perizzites, the Hivites, and the Jebusites. The cry of the Israelites has now come to me; I have also seen how the Egyptians oppress them. So come, I will send you to Pharaoh to bring my people, the Israelites, out of Egypt.' But Moses said to God, 'Who am I that I should go to Pharaoh, and bring the Israelites out of Egypt?' He said, 'I will be with you; and this shall be the sign for you that it is I who sent you: when you have brought the people out of Egypt, you shall worship God on this mountain.'

But Moses said to God, 'If I come to the Israelites and say to them, "The God of your ancestors has sent me to you", and they ask me, "What is his name?" what shall I say to them?' God said to Moses, 'I AM WHO I AM.' He said further, 'Thus you shall say to the Israelites, "I AM has sent me to you".' God also said to Moses, 'Thus you shall say to the Israelites, "The Lord the God of your ancestors, the God of Abraham, the God of Isaac, and the God of Jacob, has sent me to you": This is my name for ever, and this my title for all generations.'

Meditation

I can't do it, Lord,
   out of the question!
That's what I thought,
   and that's what I told him,
   eventually.
All right, so it took me a while to get to the point, I admit it,
   but would you have been any different?
It's not easy to say no when God asks you to do something,
   not easy at all.
So I hummed and ha'd a bit at first,
   hoping he'd see reason,
   realise he was asking too much of me.
I had good grounds, let's face it –
   I wasn't even a gifted speaker for a start,
   not even at the best of times,
   and before Pharaoh? –
   well, I knew I'd be a bag of nerves,
   scarcely able to put two words together to save my life.
Anyway, why should he listen to me,
   or anyone else for that matter?
He was the one in charge,
   the one calling the shots,
   so why listen to some jumped-up nobody

poking his nose in where it wasn't wanted?
But more to the point was my past record –
    I'd killed a man, remember, back there in Egypt,
    battered his head in and buried him in the sand.
A crime of passion, perhaps, if that can justify such a thing,
    yet for all that it was murder,
    and if anyone there was to recognise me
    and put two and two together,
    who's to say what the outcome might have been?
It could have spelt the end for me.
So when the excuses ran out
    and he still wouldn't take no for an answer,
    I told him straight:
    'Not me, Lord, get someone else to do it.'
But would you believe it, he was ready for that one,
    ready it seemed to counter any objection I could come up with.
So I finally gave in,
    no option left but to do it his way.
No, I didn't relish facing Pharaoh, too right,
    not with the message I had to deliver,
    but the prospect of facing God,
    having gone against his will,
    appealed still less.
And, do you know what? –
I need never have worried,
    for he gave me the words I needed when I needed them,
    courage such as I'd never have dreamt of,
    and faith to move mountains.
I went to Pharaoh eventually, not once,
    not twice,
    but ten times,
    cool as you like,
    with the same message: 'Let my people go!'
And finally, despite himself, the tyrant gave in,
    unable to battle any longer against the living God.
It took some doing, I can tell you,
    standing there that first time,
    but when God calls again,
    however daunting the challenge,
    however stacked against me the odds might seem,
    I won't think twice,
    for I realise now that whatever he may ask of you,
    he will more than help you do it.

To ponder

- To whom God gives the task, he gives the wit.
- Strength grows stronger through being tried.
- God provides for him who trusts.

To discuss

(Read the remainder of Exodus 3 before tackling the following questions.)

- Was Moses just making excuses, or did he have good reason to question his calling? What might this say to us today?
- How would you have responded in his place?
- What excuses do we make to evade God's challenge?
- Faith or realism? Are the two incompatible? If not, how do we marry them?

To consider further

Read Jeremiah 1:4-10, Luke 1:26-38 and Philippians 4:13. How do the responses to God's call we see in these passages compare with that of Moses? Which are we most like?

Prayer

Lord,
    all too often we feel daunted
    by the challenges facing us.
Whether it be the everyday pressures of life
    or the unique responsibilities of Christian discipleship,
    we feel inadequate to cope
    with the demands put upon us,
    lacking either the qualities, the courage
    or the commitment needed to meet them successfully.
Yet you have promised that whatever you call us to do,
    you will enable us to fulfil it,
    your Spirit always within us
    and your hand always beside us.
Inspire us, then, to respond in faith,
    confident that with you to support us
    no task is too hard to take on.
Amen.

16 The courage to continue _____

_____ *Moses*

I read recently about a celebrated author whose first novel was rejected 97 times before finally being accepted for publication! That takes some doing, doesn't it? – to keep on bouncing back from disappointment after disappointment. How many of us, I wonder, would have shown anything like that same determination? It's a rare gift! Yet that is precisely what we see in the story of Moses. Called to seek an audience with Pharaoh and demand the release of his fellow Israelites from slavery, he was to suffer repeated frustrations as his requests were either turned down flat or granted for a moment only to be denied later. It would have been hard enough for Moses to continue undeterred had he naturally warmed to the task in hand, but when we remember that every moment was an ordeal for him – so much so that his brother Aaron was needed for support – we realise the full extent of his dedication. No one could have blamed him had he washed his hands of the whole venture after the first few attempts; I suspect I would have done in his place! Yet, with incredible resilience, he battled on until at last success was achieved. His story is not just a memorable picture of human perseverance, but a glimpse of the God who reaches out with equal devotion to his people in every place and time, determined to set them free from all that holds them captive.

Reading – Exodus 11:1, 4-10

The Lord said to Moses, 'I will bring one more plague upon Pharaoh and upon Egypt; afterwards he will let you go from here; indeed, when he lets you go, he will drive you away . . .'

Moses said, 'Thus says the Lord: About midnight I will go out through Egypt. Every firstborn in the land of Egypt shall die, from the firstborn of Pharaoh who sits on his throne to the firstborn of the female slave who is behind the handmill, and all the firstborn of the livestock. Then there will be a loud cry throughout the whole land of Egypt, such as has never been or will ever be again. But not a dog shall growl at any of the Israelites – not at people, not at animals – so that you may know that the Lord makes a distinction between Egypt and Israel. Then all these officials of yours shall come down to me, and bow low to me, saying, "Leave us, you and all the people who follow you." After that I will leave.' And in hot anger he left Pharaoh.

The Lord said to Moses, 'Pharaoh will not listen to you, in order that my wonders may be multiplied in the land of Egypt.' Moses and Aaron performed all these wonders before Pharaoh: but the Lord hardened Pharaoh's heart, and he did not let the people of Israel go out of his land.

Meditation

I was ready to call it a day,
    to throw in the towel and give the whole thing up.
What more could I do?
I'd tried, hadn't I? –
    given my all as God had commanded –
    but despite everything,
    the words I'd spoken,
    the signs he'd given,
    it still apparently wasn't enough.
I'd been reluctant to get involved from the start,
    don't forget that,
    every audience filling me with dread,
    but I'd gone,
    and I'd kept on going,
    determined to play my part.
Only by then I wasn't so sure,
    for time and again my hopes had been raised
    only to be dashed before I knew it.
Could I take any more?
I really wasn't sure.
Perhaps I'd been mistaken all along,
    God not wanting to use me at all.
Perhaps I'd said the wrong things,
    given the wrong message,
    tried the wrong tack –
    who could say?
Whatever the reasons, I'd had enough,
    after all, how many times can a man be knocked down
    and keep on coming back for more?
Yet still I couldn't escape his call, try though I might.
He was urging me on,
    back to the same place
    with the same message

on the same mission.
And suddenly, I had my answer,
    for our prayer was answered –
    an end to the long years of slavery,
    freedom at last!
I was a celebrity after that,
    for a time anyway, until the next crisis came along.
And yes, if I'm honest, I was proud of what I'd achieved,
    for it hadn't come easy to me,
    not easy at all.
Yet you won't find me getting carried away,
    for I know had it been left to me alone
    it would have been a very different story,
    and a much less happy ending.
I'd have given up long before, sooner rather than later,
    our deliverance still but a dream.
No, it's not me who deserves the glory –
    it's God,
    for while *I* cared a little *he* cared completely,
    passionate enough about his people's freedom
    to keep on fighting for it
    despite the setbacks and disappointments;
    nothing finally able to withstand his purpose
    or frustrate his love.

To ponder

- If at first you don't succeed, try and try again.
- Strength grows stronger through being tried.
- Never say die.

To discuss

- It is necessary sometimes to know when to stop, but important on other occasions to persevere until we achieve our goals. How do we distinguish between such times?
- What qualities are needed if we are to battle successfully against the odds?

- What lessons do we learn when perseverance finally pays off?
- Recall instances from history of people who have bounced back successfully from disappointments (Robert the Bruce or Galileo, for example). What was it that gave them strength?

To consider further

Read Romans 8:28-39, Colossians 1:11-14 and Hebrews 12:1-2. Are there some areas of life or faith where you are in danger of giving up too easily? Have you the faith and commitment to try again, despite the disappointments of the past?

Prayer

Lord,
    it's hard to keep striving sometimes
    when all our efforts meet with failure;
    hard to keep praying
    when all our prayers seem to be unanswered;
    hard to keep believing
    when so much in life seems to undermine our faith.
Yet it is at such times as those
    that we need to hold firmly to you,
    discovering the strength that you alone can give
    and trusting in your sovereign purpose.
Teach us to persevere
    even when the odds seem hopelessly stacked against us,
    confident that your will shall finally prevail
    despite all which conspires against it.
Help us to know
    that though we may be tempted to give up on you,
    you will never give up on us!
Amen.

17 Faith in adversity _____

_____ *Moses*

We talk sometimes of experiencing a roller-coaster of emotions, and if ever that phrase was appropriate it must surely be in describing the story of the crossing of the Red Sea. Imagine, if you can, the astonishing mixture of feelings those involved must have gone through. First suspense and excitement as, after so many disappointments, they left Egypt; out into an unknown but exciting future. But then dread, dismay and despondency as it became apparent that Pharaoh had changed his mind and the Egyptians were coming after them. Next, sheer amazement at the sight of the waters opening before them, and finally, having crossed safely to the other side, an overwhelming sense of relief and exultation. There is a lesson for us here. Life does not always go smoothly, no matter how great our faith may be. It brings its fair share of challenges, even times when the future looks hopeless, but, come what may, God is with us, in both the good and the bad, the ups and the downs. Remember that next time trouble strikes. Whatever the obstacle confronting you, God is able to lead you safely through.

Reading: Exodus 14:8-14, 21-28

The Lord hardened the heart of Pharaoh king of Egypt and he pursued the Israelites, who were going out boldly. The Egyptians pursued them, all Pharaoh's horses and chariots, his chariot drivers and his army; they overtook them camped by the sea, by Pi-hahiroth, in front of Baal-zephon.

As Pharaoh drew near, the Israelites looked back, and there were the Egyptians advancing on them. In great fear the Israelites cried out to the Lord. They said to Moses, 'Was it because there were no graves for us in Egypt that you have taken us away to die in the wilderness? What have you done to us, bringing us out of Egypt? Is this not the very thing we told you in Egypt, "Let us alone and let us serve the Egyptians"? For it would have been better for us to serve the Egyptians than to die in the wilderness.' But Moses said to the people, 'Do not be afraid, stand firm, and see the deliverance that the Lord will accomplish for you today; for the Egyptians whom you see today you shall never see again. The Lord will fight for you, and you have only to keep still.'

Then Moses stretched out his hand over the sea. The Lord drove the sea back by a strong east wind all night, and turned the sea into dry land; and the waters were divided. The Israelites went into the sea on dry ground, the waters forming a wall for them on their right and their left. The Egyptians pursued them, and went into the sea after them, all of Pharaoh's horses, chariots, and chariot drivers. At the morning watch the Lord in the pillar of fire and cloud looked down upon the Egyptian army, and threw the Egyptian army into panic. He clogged the chariot wheels so that they turned with difficulty. The Egyptians said, 'Let us flee from the Israelites, for the Lord is fighting for them against Egypt.'

Then the Lord said to Moses, 'Stretch out your hand over the sea, so that the water may come back upon the Egyptians, upon their chariots and chariot drivers. So Moses stretched out his hand over the sea, and at dawn the sea returned to its normal depth. As the Egyptians fled before it, the Lord tossed the Egyptians into the sea. The waters returned and covered the chariots and chariot drivers, the entire army of Pharaoh that had followed them into the sea; not one of them remained.

Meditation

It was the *worst* moment of my life –
    that sudden desperate shout,
    and then the dust rising in the distance,
    the dull but unmistakable thud of hooves,
    and the sight of that mighty army appearing over the horizon.
We knew what it meant immediately,
    and our blood ran cold –
    the Egyptians were coming!
And then the shouting started,
    sounds I will never forget –
    the screams of terror,
    the howls of disbelief,
    the explosions of anger –
    our mood changing from one of celebration to panic,
    from unbridled joy to utter, abject despair.
I wanted to cry out too,
    my fear as acute as any,
    but I couldn't, could I? –
    not as the one who'd brought them out there,
    the one who'd got them into such a hopeless mess.
I had to seem strong,
    cool, calm, collected,

even if I didn't feel it.
But inside my stomach was churning,
    for our situation looked hopeless,
      destined to be cut down there in the wilderness,
      our brief taste of freedom ruthlessly terminated.
No wonder some of them chose to curse me,
    for I'd promised them a new beginning,
    a fresh start,
    only to lead them out there to their deaths.
How could God let it happen?
What did he think he was doing?
I shouldn't have asked, I know, but I couldn't help it.
How could he have brought us this far,
    only to abandon us now?
It couldn't be.
Somehow,
    some way,
    he would surely help us.
And then the idea came to me,
    ridiculous,
    impossible,
    unthinkable,
    yet there was no doubt in my mind
    that it was the voice of God urging us forward.
We were to cross the sea,
    to walk through the water
    and on to liberty!
Yes, I told you it sounded ridiculous,
    but I knew better than to argue,
    for time and again God had confounded our expectations,
    making the impossible look easy.
So I stretched out my hand as the Lord commanded,
    and the waters parted,
    as if rolled back by some hidden hand –
    a sight more stunning than any you could ever hope to see –
    and there before us a valley between the waves,
    a pathway to liberty.
We walked spellbound,
    eyes wide,
    mouths agape,
    hearts pounding,
    scarcely daring to breathe,
But then we were over,

the last of us safely across,
   and as I turned and stretched out my hands again
   the waters broke on our pursuers,
   a mighty torrent,
   a thundering, awesome cascade,
   crashing over their heads and sweeping them away.
We stood for a moment gazing in wonder,
   unable to take in what had happened.
But then the truth sank home,
   the reality of our deliverance,
   and we were leaping like new-born lambs,
   skipping for joy,
   running,
   laughing,
   dancing,
   unable to contain our jubilation.
The Lord had heard our cry
   and delivered us from the Egyptians;
   we were set free,
   our slavery over,
   safe at last.
And yes, I have to say it –
   it was the *best* day of my life!

To ponder

- The tree that God plants, no wind hurts it.
- Where God will help, nothing does harm.
- That never ends ill which begins in God's name.
- They are well guided that God guides.
- Faith can move mountains *(based on Matthew 17:21)*
- Great things are done when men and mountains meet; this is not done by jostling in the street. *(Gnomic Verses)*

To discuss

- Are there times when God has overcome seemingly immovable obstacles in your path? What were these? How did God help you?
- The initial response of the Israelites to the sight of the Egyptians

pursuing them was to turn on Moses and blame him for their plight. Do you see parallels here with the way you respond to crises? In what ways do you act similarly?

- What fears do you find it hardest to overcome? What response was asked of the Israelites faced by the crisis before them? What might this have to say to you?

To consider further

Read Mark 4:35-41 and Colossians 1:11-13. Let go of those fears which trouble you and put your trust in God who is able to deliver you from every danger.

Prayer

Lord,
    it is easy to follow you when life is going well;
    much harder when we come up against problems.
Our faith then evaporates so quickly,
    and we find ourselves overwhelmed by confusion,
    consumed by doubt,
    uncertain where to turn next.
Forgive us for the weakness of our faith,
    for being fair-weather disciples,
    swift to turn when the going gets rough.
Help us to recognise
    that there are times when we must face challenges
    and overcome apparently insurmountable obstacles,
    and teach us that you are as much there
    in moments such as those
    as at any other time.
Give us courage to trust in you always
    and walk wherever you might lead,
    confident that you will never fail us or forsake us.
Amen.

18 A God of our own making

Aaron

Of all the offences against God it is possible to commit, few are censured more frequently in the Old Testament than the worship of idols. Throughout its pages a succession of leaders and prophets pour scorn on anybody foolish enough to pay homage to an inanimate object fashioned by human hands, and, reading their scathing condemnations, it is tempting to imagine we could never make a similar mistake, the very idea unthinkable. Yet such self-righteousness is ill-advised, for though we would never consciously consider worshipping a man-made idol, there are insidious ways in which we do just that. The idols of our time are not carved in wood or moulded in metal, but they are no less real – money, success, power and sex are just a few of the modern-day 'gods' which hold sway today. And though we may not like to admit it, we may figure more prominently among their devotees than we care to admit. All too easily we shape our understanding of God to fit with what we want to believe. The result may seem more comfortable to live with, but in the final analysis it offers nothing, for, quite simply, we are left with no God at all.

Reading – Exodus 24:12-13, 18; 32:1-8, 19-20, 35

The Lord said to Moses, 'Come up to me on the mountain, and wait there; and I will give you the tablets of stone, with the law and the commandment, which I have written for their instruction. So Moses went up . . . into the mountain of God. Moses was on the mountain for forty days and forty nights.

When the people saw that Moses delayed to come down from the mountain, the people gathered around Aaron, and said to him, 'Come, make gods for us, who shall go before us; as for this Moses, the man who brought us up out of the land of Egypt, we do not know what has become of him.' Aaron said to them, 'Take off the gold rings that are on the ears of your wives, your sons, and your daughters, and bring them to me.' So all the people took off the gold rings from their ears, and brought them to Aaron. He took the gold from them, formed it in a mould, and cast an image of a calf; and they said, 'These are your gods, O Israel, who brought you up out of the land of Egypt!' When Aaron saw this, he built an altar before it; and Aaron made proclamation and said, 'Tomorrow shall be a festival to the Lord.' They rose early the next day, and offered burnt offerings and brought sacrifices of well-being; and the people sat down to eat and drink, and rose up to revel.

The Lord said to Moses, 'Go down at once! Your people, whom you brought up out of the land of Egypt, have acted perversely; they have been quick to turn aside from the way that I commanded them; they have cast for themselves an image of a calf, and have worshipped it and sacrificed to it, and said, "These are your gods, O Israel, who brought you up out of the land of Egypt!"'

As soon as he came near the camp and saw the calf and the dancing, Moses' anger burned hot, and he threw the tablets from his hands and broke them at the foot of the mountain. He took the calf that they had made, burned it with fire, ground it to powder, scattered it on the water, and made the Israelites drink it.

Then the Lord sent a plague on the people, because they made the calf – the one that Aaron made.

Meditation

What on earth was I thinking of?
How could I have been so foolish?
It's all a blur now, looking back,
 a grim and ghastly memory.
But it was real at the time,
 and I curl up in shame at the merest mention of it.
I must have been out of my mind,
 driven to distraction by the constant carping,
 the incessant complaints,
 but though that may explain, it can never excuse –
 not a folly as deep as mine.
It's just that they were growing desperate,
 restlessness giving way to panic
 as the hours ticked by and still no sign of Moses.
What was he up to, I wondered?
How much longer could he need up that blessed mountain?
And that's when the doubts got to me too,
 a sneaking suspicion taking hold
 that he wouldn't come back,
 some fate having surely befallen him.
I should have waited, I know that,
 but it's easy to say that with hindsight;
 for me there, on the spot, it was a different story.
I had to rebuild confidence,
 calm things down somehow,

and what better way than a visible symbol,
   tangible proof that all was well.
That's all I wanted to do, believe me,
   to make the unseen, seen,
   the unknown, known –
   the idea of building an idol was the last thing on my mind.
Yet that's what it amounted to, there's no denying it.
And you can guess what happened next, can't you?
Exactly. Trust Moses to return then of all times,
   as we knelt in worship offering our sacrifices.
You should have seen the look he gave us,
   from the face of an angel when he arrived
   to a face like thunder;
   not just anger in his eyes,
   but horror, disgust, disappointment.
Not that I could blame him,
   for he'd met God there on that mountain,
   the God of Abraham, Isaac and Jacob,
   Lord of heaven and earth.
He'd glimpsed his glory,
   heard his voice, and received his word –
   the sacred covenant engraved in stone –
   and here we were, grovelling before a lump of metal,
   flouting the most important commandment of all:
   to love the Lord our God with heart and mind and soul,
   and have no other gods before him.
It was a day to forget,
   the most humiliating moment of my life,
   and I was lucky to escape unscathed –
   many didn't.
But it wasn't wasted, not entirely,
   for as I watched that image I'd made being ground to dust,
   I remembered that, from the dust of the ground,
   God had made me,
   each one of us fashioned by his hand,
   created in his likeness, formed by his power.
To think I presumed to shape him with human hands –
   what on earth was I thinking of!

To ponder

- God is above all.
- He that is of all religions is of none.

- Only a fool tries to get the heavens into his head; the wise man is quite content to get his head into the heavens. *(G. K. Chesterton, adapted)*

To discuss

- Why do you think Aaron made the golden calf in this story? What was wrong with his actions?
- What things do we put our trust in, other than God?
- It's almost commonplace today to observe that we have turned such things as money, possessions and success into idols. But is it not equally possible that those of us who claim to worship God are guilty sometimes of fashioning him in our own image?

To consider further

Read 1 Kings 18:17-40 and Isaiah 46:5-11. What do these two passages clearly bring out concerning the folly of worshipping idols instead of serving the living God, Lord of heaven and earth?

Prayer

Sovereign God,
 you are the Creator of all,
 the Lord of history,
 ruler over space and time.
You are greater than our minds can fathom,
 your ways not our ways
 nor your thoughts our thoughts.
You alone deserve praise and worship.
Yet all too often, without realising it,
 we pay homage to other gods,
 idols of material wealth and worldly satisfaction
 which have no power to satisfy.
Forgive us for our folly,
 for inadvertently bringing you down to our level
 and losing sight of who you are.
Help us to open our lives
 to your living and searching presence,
 and so may we honour you
 in all we are and all we do.
Amen.

19 Glimpsing the promised land

Moses

Faith, we are told, is one of the great qualities of the Christian life; an essential ingredient of genuine discipleship. But living with faith is far from easy, for most of us prefer cast-iron certainties to promises we must accept on trust. Nowhere is this more so than when it comes to the fact of death and our hope of eternal life. We believe in the resurrection and the kingdom of heaven, but we can't help wishing we knew a bit more about it. Where will it be? How will we get there? When will it come? What will it be like? These and a host of other questions play on our minds, insidiously undermining our confidence. 'If only we knew,' we tell ourselves. 'If only we could see, then it would all be so much easier.' But the fact is we do not need to see anything more than God has already revealed, for true faith should be based on what we experience today as much as what we're promised tomorrow. When God is an ever-present reality in our lives we need no proofs as to the future. It is here we discover the secret of Moses, a man who, like Abraham before him, walked with God. He wasn't, of course, thinking in terms of the kingdom of heaven or of eternal life, for such beliefs did not take shape until many years afterwards, but there can be no better example of the trust we need to have in God's purpose and of the awareness that his kingdom is something we can have a foretaste of here and now.

Reading – Deuteronomy 34:1-5

Then Moses went up from the plains of Moab to Mount Nebo, to the top of Pisgah, which is opposite Jericho, and the Lord showed him the whole land: Gilead as far as Dan, all Naphtali, the land of Ephraim and Manasseh, all the land of Judah as far as the Western Sea, the Negeb, and the Plain – that is, the valley of Jericho, the city of palm trees – as far as Zoar. The Lord said to him, 'This is the land of which I swore to Abraham, to Isaac, and to Jacob, saying, "I will give it to your descendants"; I have let you see it with your eyes, but you shall not cross over there.' Then Moses, the servant of the Lord, died there in the land of Moab, at the Lord's command.

Meditation

I've seen it!
After all this time I've seen the promised land!
At a distance, true,
    just the briefest of glimpses,
    yet to me the most beautiful sight in the world.
You see, I'd longed for that moment as long as I can remember,
    the thought of it keeping me going across the years.
When my spirit sagged and my body ached,
    when my patience was tested and my nerve began to fail,
    that hope was always there to spur us on –
    the land which God had promised.
Would it have mattered if I hadn't made it,
    if I hadn't caught a snatch before I died?
I don't think so,
    for though the details were sketchy
    and the picture sometimes blurred,
    the goal was always clear enough,
    imprinted on my mind not as some futuristic kingdom
    but an ever-present reality.
God had been with me, each moment, each step,
    his love and guidance ever sure,
    so I'd lived every day as it came,
    content to leave the next in his hands,
    confident that whatever it might bring
    it was more special,
    more wonderful,
    than I could even begin to contemplate.
Not that it was always easy, I'm not saying that,
    for inevitably there were questions,
    times when it was hard to keep believing
    as the years went by and the journey unfolded.
So yes, I had my moments, as anyone would,
    and I'd have liked to see more, of course I would –
    to have set foot in those fertile fields
    and tasted the milk and honey,
    all questions answered,
    all details clear.
But I'm not complaining,
    for I *have* seen it,
    a glimpse perhaps, but enough and more than enough.
God has led me to the gates of his kingdom,
    led me the whole way through,

and I know now, if I ever doubted it before,
  his promise will not fail.
What more could I ask!

To ponder

- The best way to travel is towards heaven.
- Life is a journey, not a destination.
- Have God and have all.
- God knows well which are the best pilgrims.
- If God does not give us what we want he gives us what we need.

To discuss

- 'Like anybody else, I would like to live a long life. Longevity has its place. But I'm not concerned about that now. I just want to do God's will. And he's allowed me to go up to the mountain. And I've looked over, and I've seen the promised land. I may not get there with you, but I want you to know tonight that we as a people will get to the promised land. So I'm happy tonight. I'm not worried about anything. I'm not fearing any man. Mine eyes have seen the glory of the coming of the Lord.' The timeless words of Martin Luther King, spoken so shortly before his tragic death. What do you think Luther King meant by the promised land in this context. How far does his attitude help us to understand how Moses must have felt as he looked across the Jordan into Canaan?
- Do we conceive the kingdom to be at a time and place in the future, or equally as somewhere achievable, at least in part, here and now?

To consider further

Consider the following two passages: Luke 17:20-21 and Hebrews 11:8-16. What picture of the kingdom of God do these give? Do we make room for both perspectives in our understanding of faith?

Prayer

Lord,
 you call us to live by faith, not by sight.
You tell us to trust in things unseen,
 realities we cannot grasp.
We do our best, Lord, but it's not easy,
 for we like to have everything cut and dried,
 spelt out for us down to the finest detail.
It's true of everyday matters,
 the routine business of life,
 let alone our eternal destiny.
Yet we know deep down there is no other way,
 for the joys you hold in store for us
 are beyond our imagining,
 too awesome for the human mind to comprehend.
Teach us, then, to leave all things in your hands,
 trusting for tomorrow
 through what we know of you today.
Teach us to work for your kingdom
 until that day we enter ourselves
 into the wonder of your presence.
Amen.

20 Responding in faith

Joshua

Anyone who has ever been hill-walking will know the experience of thinking they are nearing the summit, only to find, when they get closer, that there is another stretch to climb . . . and another . . . and another! However far we progress, there is always that little bit further to go. So it proved, in a rather different sense, for Joshua and the people of Israel following the death of Moses. After years of wandering in the wilderness they had finally arrived at the border of the promised land, their long journey at last over. Or was it? A closer inspection revealed that this new land pledged to them had already been claimed by others. The task of making it their own had only just begun. No wonder Joshua, the newly chosen leader of Israel, felt over-whelmed by the sudden responsibility thrust upon him. His was the onerous challenge of rallying a people reeling from disappointment, and inspiring them to new levels of enthusiasm and endeavour. Alone, he couldn't have done it; but he wasn't alone, for God had promised to be with him wherever he went. He goes on making that promise to us today – to anyone and everyone willing to serve him.

Reading – Joshua 1:1-9

After the death of Moses the servant of the Lord, the Lord spoke to Joshua son of Nun, Moses' assistant, saying, 'My servant Moses is dead. Now proceed to cross the Jordan, you and all this people, into the land that I am giving them, to the Israelites. Every place that the sole of your foot will tread upon I have given to you, as I promised to Moses. From the wilderness and the Lebanon as far as the great river, the river Euphrates, all the land of the Hittites, to the Great Sea in the west shall be your territory. No one shall be able to stand against you all the days of your life. As I was with Moses, so I will be with you; I will not fail you or forsake you. Be strong and courageous; for you shall put this people in possession of the land that I swore to their ancestors to give them. Only be strong and very courageous, being careful to act in accordance with all the law that my servant Moses commanded you; do not turn from it to the right hand or to the left, so that you may be successful wherever you go. This book of the law should not depart out of your mouth; you shall meditate on it day and night, so that you may be careful to act in accordance with all that is written in it. For then you shall make your way prosperous, and then you shall be successful. I hereby command you: Be strong and courageous;

do not be frightened or dismayed, for the Lord your God is with you wherever you go.'

Meditation

Be strong, he said,
    be very courageous,
    and I will be with you wherever you go.
It was a wonderful promise,
    an unchanging hope in an uncertain world,
    and I needed that then, more than I can tell you.
For suddenly I was on my own, or that's how it seemed;
    our leader, Moses, taken from us,
    man of God,
    man of the people,
    man we would see no more.
He'd be a hard act to follow,
    we'd realised that from the beginning,
    each of us dreading the day
    when the end must finally come,
    but when it did I never dreamt for a moment
    I'd be the one they'd turn to,
    the one chosen by the great man himself.
I felt lost,
    bewildered –
    we all did –
    a ship without a rudder,
    an ox without a yoke.
For he'd always been there, as long as we could remember,
    leading us safely on through thick and thin.
And we'd made it, so we thought,
    our destination reaching out to greet us,
    a land flowing with milk and honey,
    peace, prosperity, at last.
Only it wasn't,
    for though the journey was over
    the conquest had just begun,
    and I was petrified,
    overwhelmed by the scale of the challenge,
    awed by the responsibility.
Who was I to take it on? –
    nothing special,
    no one gifted,
    a plain ordinary man

with a quite extraordinary mission.
I couldn't have done it,
   not alone,
   no way.
But I didn't have to, of course,
   for God was with us as he promised,
   every step of the way;
   there to challenge,
   there to guide,
   there to bless.
When my spirit failed, he was with me,
   when my foot slipped, he picked me up,
   always helping,
   always leading,
   a never-failing stream of love.
He asked one thing, that's all,
   and it wasn't much,
   hard though we found it,
   often though we failed.
It was to stay true to the commandments he had given
   in the book of the Law,
   holding them fast in our minds,
   meditating on them day and night –
   never swerving,
   never turning,
   but walking in faith, come what may.
We had our moments, like I say,
   still do, sadly –
   even now some people looking back with regret
   and ahead with consternation.
Well, it's up to them, I've done my bit –
   it's their choice, no one else's –
   but as for me and my family,
   there's no question,
   no doubt in our minds:
   we will serve the Lord.

Reading – Joshua 24:15-17a, 18b

'Now if you are unwilling to serve the Lord, choose this day whom you will serve, whether the gods your ancestors served in the region beyond the River or the gods of the Amorites in whose land you are living; but as for me and my household, we will serve the Lord.' Then the people answered, 'Far be it from us that we should forsake the

Lord to serve other gods; for it is the Lord our God who brought us and our ancestors up from the land of Egypt, out of the house of slavery . . . Therefore we also will serve the Lord, for he is our God.'

To ponder

- Great things are done more through courage than through wisdom.
- The weapon of the brave is in his heart.
- A door must either be shut or open.
- Courage and perseverance conquer all before them.

To discuss

- What do you find hardest about Christian commitment?
- What experiences in life present the greatest challenge to our faith, and why?
- Where do you look to for guidance and strength? What have you found most effective in times of crisis or uncertainty?

To consider further

Read Matthew 28:16-20 and Hebrews 11:32-39. In the light of these verses, reflect upon situations in your life where you feel at the end of your tether.

Prayer

Lord,
    it's hard to bounce back from disappointment,
    to find new reserves and fresh inspiration
    to try and try again.
When we've given our all
    and believe we've achieved something,
    when we've kept on battling
    despite the obstacles in our way,
    it hurts to accept that there are still more hurdles to face,
    yet more setbacks to overcome.
Yet though we may sometimes feel weary at the demands,
    we know in our hearts that life is made of such challenges;
    no achievement, however special,
    sufficient to answer all our dreams.
Renew us, then, through your Holy Spirit,
    and give us the faith and commitment we need
    to live each day as your pilgrim people,
    pressing on towards the prize.
Amen.

Final Prayer

Living God,
  for all the times we have wrestled against you,
  flouting your will,
  ignoring your call,
  disobeying your commandments,
  resisting your guidance,
  forgive us.

In all the times we wrestle with you,
  striving to understand more,
  searching for meaning,
  grappling with our unbelief,
  begging for your help,
  hear us.

In all the times we wrestle in faith,
  seeking to do your will,
  working towards your kingdom,
  committing ourselves to your service,
  confronting evil and injustice in your name,
  bless us.

Teach us not to contend *against* you
  but to work *with* you,
  to grapple earnestly with the great mysteries of faith,
  and to give of ourselves freely in the cause of Christ.

Go with us we pray,
  and may your word live within us,
  a lamp for our path
  and a fire on our tongue,
  to the glory of your name.

Amen.

Index of Bible passages

(References are to meditation rather than page numbers)

Index of principal characters _____

Index of principal themes _____